ON WHITMAN

WRITERS ON WRITERS

Philip Lopate | *Notes on Sontag*

C. K. Williams | *On Whitman*

C. K. WILLIAMS 🔲 **ON WHITMAN**

PRINCETON UNIVERSITY PRESS

Princeton and Oxford

Copyright © 2010 by Princeton University Press

Published by Princeton University Press, 41 William Street,
Princeton, New Jersey 08540

In the United Kingdom: Princeton University Press, 6 Oxford Street,
Woodstock, Oxfordshire OX20 1TW

press.princeton.edu

Library of Congress Cataloging-in-Publication Data
Williams, C. K. (Charles Kenneth), 1936–
    On Whitman / C. K. Williams.
        p. cm.—(Writers on writers)
    ISBN 978-0-691-14472-6 (cloth : alk. paper)
    1. Whitman, Walt, 1819–1892—Criticism and interpretation.
    2. Whitman, Walt, 1819–1892—Influence.   I. Title.
    PS3238.W57 2010
    811'.3—dc22   2009040347

British Library Cataloging-in-Publication Data is available

This book has been composed in Minion and Myriad.
Printed on acid-free paper. ∞
Printed in the United States of America
10 9 8 7 6 5 4 3 2 1

▣ CONTENTS

When I mentioned to a poet-friend that I was thinking of writing a small book on Whitman, he answered, "What in heavens name is left to say?"—a very reasonable question. The mass of commentary on Whitman, on Whitman's poems, Whitman's America, Whitman's world, is all but overwhelming. A bibliography of the germane commentary on the poetry would make a large volume in itself; a consideration of the work that attempts to situate the man in his time and place would make another. To mention just my two of my favorite books: Paul Zweig's *Walt Whitman: The Making of the Poet* is a sensitive, erudite poet's probing of the unlikeliness of a phenomenon like *Leaves of Grass* being generated by what to all appearances was a rather mediocre journalist and sometime lecturer in the disorganized turbulence of nineteenth-century Brooklyn and Manhattan. And David S. Reynolds's *Walt Whitman's America* is a meticulous, comprehensive, and illuminating study of the culture and the civilization from which Whitman and his poems were brought forth: it's an inspired consideration of many too little noticed aspects of nineteenth-century American life and an indispensable companion to the poet's work.

Over the course of my writing life and in preparing to write this book, I've read—not at all systematically to be sure—quite a lot on Whitman. But it recently occurred to me that there was something I was no longer enjoying in reading what has been said about the sources and the purposes of Whitman's poetry. Paradoxical as it might seem, in preparing this book I just didn't any longer want to balance against the work the marvelous insights in the Zweig and Reynolds books, for instance, about Whitman's devotion to opera, or to oration, or to the half-cracked science of phrenology which nonetheless nourished him with so many images and terms. As useful as their research has been in situating Whitman's work in its time and place, all of it is finally reabsorbed into the sheer, ever amazing power of the poems themselves.

Even more oddly perhaps, I didn't particularly want to revisit the mass of what Whitman himself had to pronounce about his grand intentions and ambitions for his poetry. I don't mean to say that I'm not glad to have been exposed to all of it, but I felt the need to clear the air—to approach the poetry as I had when I first came across it, to try to reestablish and reconfirm the raw power of the poetry in the context it was making for itself on the page, not in the range of all that lay behind it.

For a young poet, reading Whitman is sheer revelation, sheer wonder, a delight bordering on then plunging into disbelief. How could all this have come to pass? This stupendous, relentless surge of poetic music with its intricate and constantly surprising combinations of sound? These countless images of daily life, of common life made uncommon, and the most boldly uncommon made jarringly intimate? Whitman's audacious eschatological and metaphysical speculations were precious to him, yet so precisely and judiciously are they embodied and embedded in his poetry that they end up being more feasible than most or, for some of us, any religious texts.

It's the poetry, though, the poetry, poetry, poetry that continues to astonish and inspire. Emerson said of Michelangelo that "he builded better than he knew," and, wise and engrossing as the man was who wrote the prefaces and recollections of composing *Leaves of Grass*, this seems undeniably and almost tautologically the case with Whitman.

Whitman's inspiration, and his enactment of that inspiration, is inimitable and seemingly inexhaustible. For me, the only other poet with whom he can compare this way is Shakespeare, if clearly for different reasons. With both poets, I never turn away from them because I've even temporarily exhausted my response to their work, but because I feel my own limits in relation with them. With both, but particularly with Whitman, I need a respite, surcease, so as not to be overwhelmed, obliterated. This is more raw than Bloom's "anxiety of influence," more primitive: there's no question of influence here, it's more a colonization, an evaporation, the fear that if I give myself over too completely to him, my own poet will be annihilated, that I'll become a mere acolyte, a follower, an appendage—a terrible nightmare, from which Whitman's poems themselves thank goodness awaken me yet again.

I have tried in this book, with much digression to be sure, and with unavoidable and finally grateful reference to some of Whitman's commentators, to go back to the *Leaves of Grass* to explore what it is that continues to inspire and sometimes daunt me about Whitman's singular masterpiece.

There were a number of editions of *Leaves of Grass*, from the original version in 1855 to the so-called deathbed edition of 1891–92. As I've pointed out, Whitman continued to revise the book throughout his life, altering poems and adding a large number. For a long time after his death, it was assumed that the final edition should be authoritative; it was, after all, Whitman's last word, and in the vast majority of cases an author's accumulated revisions are improvements and accepted as definitive.

But for Whitman, this just isn't so. In 1959 Malcolm Cowley republished the 1855 edition, with an introduction convincingly proclaiming that it (and particularly the first as yet then untitled section later called "Song of Myself") was Whitman's greatest work, and most poets, scholars, and readers have agreed.

In my view, and in that of the poets I know, many of the changes Whitman made in later editions diluted and diffused his first brilliant inspiration. By the time of the deathbed edition, he had tinkered so much with some of the poems that though they're still recognizable, reading them beside the earlier versions can be disheartening, even shocking. Whitman in an 1890 letter says: "The writing and rounding . . . of L of G, has been to me the reason-for-being, & life comfort." What he meant by "rounding" was revising, tinkering, which, though it helped his mood and probably to pass time, was sometimes unfortunate for the work.

Whitman himself said of the book, "that former and main volume," that it was "composed in the flush of my health and strength, from the age of 30 to 50 years," and yet he continued to put it through his mill long after his poetic powers had deteriorated. This is a sad thing to say about any artist, but a side-by-side reading of the different versions makes it undeniable.

Given all this, unless otherwise noted, I have quoted throughout from the 1855 versions of the poems, except in regard to their titles—the sections of the first edition had none, and the ones the poems have come to be known by—"I Sing the Body Electric," for instance—were added later. With poems from the later editions, I've used the versions that seem to me, frankly, to be most inspired, most accomplished, and I've noted in which edition they appeared.

Would Whitman have been offended? Not the younger Whitman, certainly, who wasn't yet considered by his admirers and didn't yet consider himself an institution.

As for which editions I'd recommend: besides any of the several current publications of the 1855 edition, of the shorter selections I'd suggest Galway Kinnell's *The Essential Whitman*, a great poet's personal line-by-line culling and reassembling of the best of the poetry. A more expansive selection, Gary Schmidgall's *Walt Whitman: Selected Poems 1855–1892*, collects the first versions of many of the great poems, including all of the 1855 edition, and I find this a useful collection for a broader sampling. On the other hand, the earlier versions of the poems aren't invariably the best. For example, "Out of the Cradle Endlessly Rocking," with its incomparable title repeated as the first line, in its first appearance in the 1860 edition was called "A Word Out of the Sea," without the first line.

The Library of America edition, *Walt Whitman: Complete Poetry and Collected Prose*, includes the entirety of the 1891–92 deathbed edition, which is as I say sometimes diluted and even despoiled by Whitman's unfortunate revisings. But it does include the whole of the 1855 edition, and a strong sampling of Whitman's prose, so it has to be the most indispensable single volume.

Very useful also is the Walt Whitman Archive, edited by Ed Folsom and Kenneth M. Price (www.whitmanarchive.org), which contains facsimiles and searchable texts of all the editions of *Leaves of Grass*.

One further remark: in writing this book, I often found myself overwhelming my text with quotations from whatever poem to which I may have been referring. To keep from finishing with a much larger volume than my publishers had in mind, I've tried to keep in check my temptation to quote copiously, assuming that anyone reading this book would keep a copy of *Leaves of Grass* at hand.

ON WHITMAN

The Music

▨ We know that as he wandered the streets, as he rode in the omnibuses, probably as he sat in lectures and in the opera, he scribbled in small notebooks and on scraps of paper he stuffed in his pockets. We know he then transcribed them, ordered them, wrote them down, then set the type for the first editions of his great work himself. . . . And there it was, on the page. . . . We know, we know, we know . . . .

"He was learning his craft," we like to think. Always with the notion of craft comes the implication of progress, improvement. The very word craft seems to have inherent in it the precept that the more you practice your art, the more you labor at it and study it, the more craft you'll have, the better you'll be able to effect your poetry, or anything else. This can be quite a debilitating credo—I've known poets who for all intents and purposes spent their life learning their art, preparing to write poems, but never getting around to actually doing it. Similarly, critics will sometimes make up a lengthy biography for poets whose precociousness seems to be a denial of the normal evolution of the attainment of knowledge. It can seem completely unfeasible to believe that

Keats or Rimbaud didn't somehow do something practical to absorb all they had to in the preparation of their poetic activities. I once read an article about Rimbaud that set out to prove that his very unlikely knowledge of so many matters of the history of poetics, and of history itself, had to have been the result of the thousands of hours he'd spent in the Bibliothèque Nationale, sneaking off presumably from the rather bohemian time-wasting that comprised most of the actual life of the seventeen-year-old he was when he wrote his greatest poems.

Whitman's craft, his skill, was supreme during that first blazing burst when he was compiling the 1855 edition of *Leaves of Grass* and adding to it in the nearly as inspired years afterward. But though he had been for some years a productive journalist, there's still no way really to account for how he accumulated in such a short time so many singular methods, so many facets for the expression of his talent; there was no place he could have "learned" his craft: it evolved along with his identity, with his very self.

The new way of composing must have come all at once; I imagine it must have felt like some kind of conversion experience. There are very few signs before the 1855 edition that this great thing was about to occur. It's as though his actual physical brain went through some incredible mutation, as though—a little science fiction, why not?—aliens had transported him up to their spaceship and put him down again with a new mind, a new poetry apparatus. It is really that crazy.

And, most important, we don't know where his *music* came from; though there are isolated lines in the notebooks that offer clues, we'll never really know when he first fully intuited, and heard, and knew, that surge of language sound, verse sound, that pulse, that swell, that sweep, which was to become his medium, his chariot—just to try to imagine him consciously devising it is almost as astounding as it must have been for him to discover it.

It's essential to keep in mind that in poetry the music comes first, before everything else, *everything* else: until the poem has found its music, it's merely verbal matter, information. Thought, meaning, vision, the very words, come after the music has been established, and in the most mysterious way they're already contained in it. Without the music, there's nothing; thought, merely, ideation; in Coleridge's terms, not imagination, just fancy; intention, hope, longing, but not poetry: *Wait, Muse! Let me sing it to you, wait!* That might be what drives poets to desperation, or worse: the waiting, the wanting, the sensing of the cadences, the melodies, but being unable to force them. It's also probably what tends poets towards manic-depressiveness, because when the music does finally arrive, the mix of relief and exaltation is unreal, beyond self, ego, consciousness, and conscience.

Usually the music seems to come along simultaneously with the words and the matter, but not always. Mandelstam spoke of hearing the music for a poem, feeling it, before it had any words at all. Pavese said: "By means of murmuring, I gave a rhythm to my poems." Poetry is song and language at once. Neuroscientists say now that there are separate areas in the brain, individual "modules," for one and the other. Poetry's splendor, its seduction, its addictive potential surely resides in this bringing of separate psychic realms together in one mental and emotional speech-act, thought-act. Dante has the poets in Limbo going off together alone to speak of things that are not to be revealed to others, even in his Comedy of revelation. What could these things be other than that most profound and most blatant secret of the poets: that only they can generate this unlikely marvel, language music—in great poets a music immediately recognizable and resolutely unique?

In "Song of Myself," Whitman chants aloud the secret to himself:

My voice goes after what my eyes cannot
reach,
With the twirl of my tongue I encompass
worlds and volumes of worlds.
Speech is the twin of my vision . . . . it is
unequal to measure itself.

The Past

When and how Whitman first heard his music is a mystery still, perhaps *the* mystery. What he had heard and had read meant either a great deal or, probably more likely, not terribly much. There were influential voices around him, some orators, some religious texts, that might be conceived of as generically similar to the voice he devised. There's the poet Samuel Warren, whose *The Lily and the Bee* Paul Zweig cites as having possibly influenced Whitman, but Warren's music, though metrically loose, is notably clunky and inelegant; it would have been for Whitman more of an example to be avoided then emulated.

And of course there were voices in the tradition of poetry that had to have helped him forge his language mechanism into the shape it finally achieved. Macpherson's *Ossian* is sometimes mentioned, and John Milton's work. Whitman spoke with admiration of Milton, but Milton wasn't the influence for him he had been, say, for Keats, a master, a teacher, so that some of Keats's early sonnets sound at first as though Milton might have composed them. "When I consider how my life is spent . . . ." "When I have fears that I may cease to be . . . ."

Whitman's break with the past was much more radical, more like Christopher Smart's, whose "Jubilate Agno" certainly would, in its frank assertion of verse improvisation, have offered hints to Whitman of how he came to use phrase and clause as organizing principles. But at least as far as I can discover, Whitman seems never to have heard of Smart. Blake, another radical innovator? Whitman was introduced to Blake by his adoring would be lover-wife, then good friend, Anne Gilchrist. Gilchrist, who came from England to marry Whitman but quickly realized he wasn't husband material yet stayed close to him, had completed her husband Alexander Gilchrist's biography of Blake after Alexander died, but her advent in Whitman's life was long after he had devised the music for his poems.

Many commentators compare the cadences of the poems and their use of parallelisms with those of the King James Bible, and surely those rhythms would have been resonating somewhere in Whitman's musical poetic psyche, but I'm not convinced. Whitman certainly did use some of its parallel structures, but the Bible has few instances of sentences laden with as many phrases as those with which Whitman charged his, which is one of the singular characteristics of his music. As great and influential as the King James Bible is, and as much as Whitman surely would have had to have been influenced by his experience of it, I think he used as many of Shakespeare's chromatic rhythms and rhetorics as the Bible's.

I remember long ago working for hours with some other young poets trying different systems of verse analysis that counted stressed and unstressed syllables, most notably that devised by George Stewart in his still useful *Techniques of English Verse*, that we thought might help situate Whitman in the tradition of English poetic rhythms. But *Leaves of Grass* always resisted, and, though it was fun for awhile, we never found a satisfying way to account for Whitman's finally unpredictable music. And of course there are dozens of critics who have tried to do the same thing, most successfully Gay Wilson Allen,[*] but in the end the results are always inconclusive.

There are hints about Whitman's sources, though: poets in the throes of precomposition will often resort to existing poems—usually great ones but not always—to inaugurate, impel, a sound, a movement, any sound, any movement, beyond the obdurate plod of prose. Sometimes this glance to other poetry works, though oddly enough the music that begins to be realized will often bear no resemblance to the winged Pegasus that led the way. With Whitman, because the evidence is so meager, there's a point at which we have to have recourse to the notion of "genius." Art most often evolves in what appear to be cautious increments, but there are those figures who innovate more quickly and forcefully and ultimately mysteriously than that.

We have to give Whitman's genius its due: he did something that the evidence is in no way able

[*] In *A Reader's Guide to Walt Whitman* (New York: Farrar Straus and Giroux, 1970).

to predict no matter how scrupulously we scour through his predecessors. It's reasonable to try to account for the innovations *Leaves of Grass* makes, but at some point all that speculation has to be suspended so we can simply appreciate with gratitude the huge gift Whitman made to the universe of poetry. As with certain other geniuses—Shakespeare, Dante, Homer—his sources are simply absorbed, or wrenched, into the sheer originality of the poetry. If we are to use the term "influence" about Whitman, what's most remarkable is the influence his work more than any other poet's has had on poets all over the world, rather than that which may or may not have conditioned his own work.

Let that initial gasp of amazement at the splendor of the work lead us to the exhalation of gratitude that all this could have come about.

Beginnings

We'll never know either what the lines were in which Whitman first heard his music. The lines that begin the poem?

> *I celebrate myself,*
> *And what I assume you shall assume,*

> *For every atom belong to me as good belongs*
> *to you.*

Perhaps, though it doesn't feel likely somehow. Turn to any page in that first *Leaves of Grass* . . .

> *I hear you whispering there O stars of heaven,*
> *O suns . . . . O grass of graves . . . . O perpetual*
> *transfers and promotions . . . . if you do*
> *not say anything how can I say anything?*

That? Why not? Poets traditionally look to the stars, don't they? And look to the ground then, and in the ground is death. Or this:

> *I have heard what the talkers were talking . . . .*
> *the talk of the beginning and the end,*
> *But I do not talk of the beginning or the end.*

And then a little leap, of sense and music.

> *There was never any more inception than*
> *there is now,*
> *Nor any more youth or age than there is now;*
> *And will never be any more perfection than*
> *there is now,*
> *Nor any more heaven or hell than there is*
> *now.*

And another abrupt tonal shift, characteristic of Whitman's work, but where did it *come* from?

> *Urge and urge and urge,*
> *Always the procreant urge of the world.*

Shiftings and leaps: unlogical, ungrounded, unconnected, from one theme, one image, one anecdote, one sound to another. Surely his original method, that gathering of scraps in notebooks and scraps in his pockets, must have gone far towards permitting—once he gave in to them—the music, and that peculiar system of connection, that wonderfully gappy unorganized organization.

If he was like other poets I know, when he felt, heard, knew that music, the first question he would have asked himself was how long he'd be able to stay in it, to, as jazz musicians say, *ride* it. The music was so forceful, so engrossing, so generative, that it couldn't have taken him long, a few instants, a few months at most, to realize he'd discovered a musical system that was magically encompassing and had within it echoes of other singings, the Bible, oratory, opera, even some older poetry, but was entirely unique as well. Then it might have taken him some other gigantic moment to realize that not only would his world, his entire world, fit within it, but that the music would take him to places of imagination and intellect and spirit he would have never have dreamed without it.

He must have been—no, surely *was*—in a state of bliss that lasted for years, through all the miserable trials of his family in the 1850s, through all the anguish of having to watch a nation prepare to sunder itself: he was still listening to his music, scribbling, assembling. He'd have *lived* within the music, exulted in it. Dizzying to think of it.

It was a music, and a musical-poetic vision, that flourished abundantly, wildly. A music so satisfying, so irrepressible that even when some twenty years or so later he realized it had left him, had left him even years before that, he expressed no great grief, though he surely had had no inkling during those early blazing years that it ever might wane. In those first years he projected the number of poems en route in the hundreds—he spoke of 365 for the third, 1860 edition—and if he didn't quite generate that number, there were still dozens and dozens of new poems, almost all splendid.

But, sadly, at some point it did go bad for him. He lost the connection to his music, not knowing at first that he had. Trying to keep it going, after the 1860s, into the '70's and '80's, he kept making new poems, but his locutions become odd and awkward, his rhythms uncertain, his diction sometimes almost primitive. As Galway Kinnell writes in the introduction to his *Essential Whitman*: "By the mid-sixties his work began to fill up with the very poeticism and archaisms he had started off by excluding—'o'er,' 'e'en,' 'erewhile,' 'i,' 'tis,' 'ope,' . . . ."

And often he couldn't in his endless tinkering and revising hear himself as he had, and he all but untuned the original power of his symphony. He was having fatal trouble sounding like himself, the poet he had been, whose music was diluted now, and weary, maybe because his body itself had begun to be prematurely sick and weary and old. In some of the later poems there are moments, too many, of a kind of dutiful ecstasy. This is a cardinal sin for artists, sham inspiration, but perhaps Whitman has to be forgiven for this because his method itself was so much involved with the ecstatic. If his inspiration sometimes no longer fulfilled the fiery needs of his method, we have to be grateful for the many times it had.

And there came a time when he knew himself he'd lost it. Speaking of a sketch someone was making of him, he was quoted as saying: "The devil in artists is to keep pegging away at a thing after it is all done—pegging away at it *done,* till it is *undone.*" Fortunately we still have those earlier, unpegged-away-with editions.

Vision

But how wildly exciting, how really exalting it must have been to him when his poetry first offered him a way to see and record so much—it can feel like *everything.* Just reading it, the brilliance of the moments of inspiration are like raw synaptic explosions, like flashbulbs going off in the brain, in the mind: pop, pop, pop. The images, the ideas, the visions, the insights, the proclamations, the stacks of brilliant verbal conjunctions, the musical inventiveness and uniqueness: one after the other, again and again, in a form that reveals them naked, unmodulated, undimmed by any apparent resort to the traditional resources of poetic artfulness. Reading it, being in it, as in the work of terribly few poets, there's a kind of inspirational elation: the world in the poems and the world we live in, the cosmos that's ours—all of it imbued with significance.

And for him . . . he walks through the streets, he stops on the seashore, he watches the city traffic, the people, the people; he thinks, he remembers, and he knows how fortunate he is, how thrilling this is. Later, in 1871, he'll write, in "Sparkles from the Wheel": *"Myself effusing and fluid—a phantom curiously floating—now where absorb'd and arrested."* That pure noticing, that registering, that accounting for, all for its own sake, and for the sake of his vision, begins a few pages into the "Song." Until then, the poem has primarily been a lengthy, digressive, poetically brilliant argument establishing the self who will be the person of the poem, what his relation with his attentive, ideal reader will be, and the images, even those that are fairly precise and seemingly off the point, are elements of that argument.

He introduces this new function of the poem at first in somewhat general terms:

> *Every kind for itself and its own . . . . for me*
> *   mine male and female,*
> *For me all that have been boys and love*
> *   women,*
> *For me the man that is proud and feels how it*
> *   stings to be slighted . . .*

Then, after the famous line (infamous, for D. H. Lawrence*) *"Who need be afraid of the merge?"* a few lines later begins the particularization that will become the mortar and underpinning of all the poem's conceptualizations. It starts with a tender scene of the poet with a child and then moves on for the first time to make definite the characters, individuals, presences who will populate from then on all the rest of Whitman's great and even lesser work.

> *The little one sleeps in its cradle,*
> *I lift the gauze and look a long time, and*
> *silently brush away flies with my hand.*

---

* Lawrence, in his quirky, heartfelt, and oddly influential book *Studies in Classic American Literature*, first loves Whitman, because he recognizes in him someone as passionate, frank, and committed to truth as he is. Then he hates him, because he thinks for a moment of Whitman's notion of "merging," which Whitman mentions a few times and which Lawrence thinks Whitman thinks is central to his work, and makes irritatingly much of it. Then he loves him again, because he's able to drop the accusations, and just read, and love, the poems again, without worrying about the dissimilarity between some of Whitman's ideas and his own. And he does love him, and despite his misgivings expresses it well, in his own Laurentian terms: "His was a morality of the soul living her life, not saving herself."

> *The youngster and the redfaced girl turn aside*
> > *up the busy hill,*
> *I peeringly view them from the top.*

("Peeringly"—what a crazily appropriate adverb.)

> *The suicide sprawls on the bloody floor of the*
> > *bedroom.*
> *It is so . . . . I witnessed the corpse . . . . there*
> > *the pistol had fallen.*

And then even the "I" can be dispensed with; only the "eye" (and ear) are necessary now.

> *The blab of the pave . . . . the tires of carts*
> > *and sluff of bootsoles and talk of the*
> > *promenaders,*
> *The heavy omnibus, the driver with interro-*
> > *gating thumb, the clank of the shod horses*
> > *on the granite floor,*
> *The carnival of sleighs, the clinking and*
> > *shouted jokes and pelts of snowballs . . .*

For the rest of his writing life, he'll be this eye, this ear, this voracious devourer of the world. Whitman sometimes compared himself (with proper humility) to Shakespeare, and edged on toward Dante and even Homer. Of course he differs radically from all three, but in this sheer largeness, this huge digestion of numberless atoms and chunks of reality, he is in their camp, is one of them, with them. A few dozen lines later he introduces the first of the many extended anecdotes and brief narratives that will become another facet of his intricately structured sprawl.

> *I saw the marriage of the trapper in the open*
> *air in the far-west . . . . the bride was a red*
> *girl,*
> *Her father and his friends sat near by cross-*
> *legged and dumbly smoking . . . . they had*
> *moccasins to their feet and large thick*
> *blankets hanging from their shoulders;*
> *On a bank lounged the trapper . . . . he was*
> *dressed mostly in skins . . . . his luxuriant*
> *beard and curls protected his neck,*
> *One hand rested on his rifle . . . . the other*
> *hand held firmly the wrist of the red girl,*
> *She had long eyelashes . . . . her head*
> *was bare . . . . her coarse straight locks*
> *descended upon her voluptuous limbs*
> *and reached to her feet.*

A vivid, moving scene—what matter if it was based on a well-known painting, *The Trapper's Bride*, by Alfred Jacob Miller? I find it nobler precisely because it is. By borrowing from Miller,

Whitman shows he is digesting not only what is before him in the world, and what he imagines, but even what he can find in the world of art and others' imaginations. The dignity in this scene of the "red girl" and the intimacy of her family and friends with the white trapper (though some refer to it as a "bondage" scene; implying the wife was being purchased, which I doubt) introduces us to the one that immediately follows, which is even more sensually depicted and has a greater moral charge.

> *The runaway slave came to my house and*
>   *stopped outside,*
> *I heard his motions crackling the twigs of the*
>   *woodpile,*
> *Through the swung half-door of the kitchen I*
>   *saw him limpsey and weak,*
> *And went where he sat on a log, and led him*
>   *in and assured him,*
> *And brought water and filled a tub for his*
>   *sweated body and bruised feet,*
> *And gave him a room that entered from my*
>   *own, and gave him some coarse clean*
>   *clothes,*
> *And remember perfectly well his revolving*
>   *eyes and his awkwardness,*

And remember putting plasters on the galls of
his neck and ankles . . . .

This, too, had to have been a fiction, or borrowing—Whitman lived then in Brooklyn with
his family, and surely without the "firelock" standing in a corner he mentions a few lines later—
but again it doesn't really matter: the enactment
of concern and compassion of the episode, its
promulgation of racial acceptance, and above all
its delicate and intimate details are ethically convincing and inspiring.

By now in the poem Whitman is purposefully
creating an edifice, in which every numberless
particle is named and accounted for. Generalizations there are, many of them, but they have the
same poetic weight as the hundreds and hundreds of precise observations; it's this balancing
and equalizing of the conceptual and the particular that makes both resonate with a peculiar and
unfamiliar richness. Sometimes the two actions
happen in startling adjacency.

Do you not know how the buds beneath are
folded?
Waiting in gloom protected by frost,
The dirt receding before my prophetical
screams.

I underlying causes to balance them at last,
My knowing my live parts . . . . it keeping tally
*   with the meaning of things . . .*

I feel tempted to go on through the pages that follow now, some of the richest in the *Leaves*, but I realize there'd be no place to stop: the sights, the sounds, the stories are inexhaustible. Turn to any page and there'll be more, more of the beauty of existence, more of the unlikeliness of language.

Where beehives range on a gray bench in the
*   garden half-hid by the high weeds;*
Where the band-necked partridges roost in a
*   ring on the ground with their heads out;*
Where burial coaches enter the arch'd gates of
*   a cemetery;*
Where winter wolves bark amid wastes of
*   snow and icicled trees . . .*

From life, to death, to life: always the churning, always the noticing without judging.

Depths

A question Whitman asked in "The Song of Myself," a question more integral to his project than it at first seems: *"Have you felt so proud to get at the meaning of poems?"* What this implies is that there are mysteries in ordinary poems, secrets that are to be decoded, depths that only the initiated can dare to or are capable of plumbing.

But in fact, what's striking is that there are no "depths" in Whitman, no secrets, no allegories, no symbols in the sense of one thing standing for another, an aspect of matter standing for an element of spirit. Everything in Whitman's poems is brought to the surface, everything is articulated, made as clear and vivid and in a way as uninterpretable as it can be. If something does stand for something else—the bird in "Out of the Cradle Endlessly Rocking," for instance, or the lilac or thrush in "When Lilacs Last in the Door-Yard Bloom'd"—he tells us, or all but tells us, it does; he makes sure that there can be no mistake about his intention. It would be foolhardy to read Whitman with an eye to Eliot's "objective correlatives"—his notion of images embodying complex ideations—because nothing in the poems answers to that definition, although everything in them serves the same function of enrichment, of layering of response. The layers are all laid out on the page: the complexity of the response that's demanded is the same Eliot described, but it's a complexity, again, an equation, all of whose parts are revealed.

This is a key element in Whitman's aesthetic, perhaps its essence. Perhaps, too, it's a part of his ambition to make a poem that would be emblematic of American democracy while at the same time embodying it. It might also help to explain Whitman's disappointment that the poem didn't have the wide reception he'd hoped and assumed it would; his surprise that the poets who still worked in an aesthetic that he characterized as "European" would receive vastly greater attention than he did.

The Man Before the Poems

▨ Both sides of the family in America for generations, quite well-off for a period, then not. Father a failed farmer in Long Island. Then failed house builder in Brooklyn, where he dragged his wife and children—eight finally, another had died in infancy—when Whitman was three or four. Whitman leaves school at eleven, works as office boy, clerk, printer's devil at a newspaper—he'd continue to work on and off at newspapers, editing some, even starting several, all through his pre-poet's life. Before that though, the family moves back to Long Island, where he tries teaching (leaves school at eleven, begins teaching at seventeen!). Hates it for the most part, feels isolated, marooned in the rural backwaters.

So, back to Brooklyn, house builder now with his still unsuccessful father, then into printing, then journalism. Enthusiastically bohemian life, bars, taverns, artists' gathering places; dives, brothels (probably as an observer). Loved opera, oratory, the streets, the rivers. Read widely, everything, indiscriminately from phrenology to Egyptian arcania; attended lectures assiduously; museums, galleries: insatiable.

Every sort of family intrigue. One brother mentally "defective," whose plight surely informed the quietly rending lines:

> *The lunatic is carried at last to the asylum a*
> *confirmed case,*
> *He will never sleep any more as he did in the*
> *cot in his mother's bedroom . . .*

Another brother a fatal drinker, leaving a widowed sister-in-law who ended up a prostitute in the streets. Loved his mother passionately through her life.

Many friends, many people he expressed love to, and for, mostly males. Was he homosexual? Surely, though later in his life some of his more narrow-minded admirers denied it, and he in an oft-quoted letter once did too, but there's no question that in the poems his most emphatic erotic passion is for men, even if sometimes it was sublimated to a kind of exalted comradeship between males. And there's certainly evidence that at least early in his life he had had homosexual experiences. Did he have affairs with women? He said so, and there's one letter from a woman that seems to imply it, but it's finally very unlikely.

Politically, he could sometimes be called radical, at other times conservative. He was anti-abolitionist, then not. Pro-war with the Mexican War, then anti- when the Civil War was looming. He was generous in his poems toward blacks but sometimes expressed in conversation the reflexive, denigrating racism of his time. He was almost everything, then not, or then at last.

Before *Leaves of Grass,* he wrote continuously: bad short stories, a temperance novel, worse, some inept early poems; a few were even published and were dreadful, unforgivably bad. Went to New Orleans with his brother to start another newspaper for someone, came back by way of the

Midwest and West; he only traveled rarely again, to Boston, to Canada, though he liked to imply in the poems he'd done much more. Now, though, New York again, again journalism, freelancing, editing; a full life again; many comrades and acquaintances, among them Edgar Allan Poe.

Then, all at once, 1855, a book, publication paid for by himself; on the title page, *Leaves of Grass*: Brooklyn, NY, 1855; nothing else, no author's name, just that etching of him in a casually opened shirt and floppy hat. We learn the author's name only halfway through the first poem—*Walt Whitman*.

> *Walt Whitman, an American, one of the*
> *roughs, a kosmos,*
> *Disorderly fleshy and sensual . . . . eating*
> *drinking and breeding,*
> *No sentimentalist . . . . no stander above men*
> *and women or apart from them . . . . no*
> *more modest than immodest.*

Walt Whitman now exists, and the poems exist, and ordinary life essentially ends for him; everything now is a function of those poems, everything that came before perceived now as a preparation for them. Everything afterwards dedication to them, obsession with them.

(Though in truth for at least a few more years he was still a youngish person with a real life, still the ego-ridden Walter. He writes in a letter from Boston, in 1860: "Every body here is so like everybody else—and I am Walt Whitman!—Yankee curiosity and cuteness, for once, is thoroughly stumped, confounded, petrified, made desperate.")

Self-Made

▦ The poet Antonio Machado once commented: "In order to write the poem, you have to invent the poet to write it," and Whitman did just that: he was, as Paul Zweig puts it, a truly self-made man, although that locution tends to imply financial independence, which Whitman never quite attained. Say instead "self-assembled." He put himself together like an inventor in a dream-shed of spare parts; he created himself; he was a *fiction*, at least at first, but such a glorious one. Enormous emotions, wild and accurate and sweeping perceptions, philosophical fancies, a kind of mad spiritual purity: he surely was, as he put it, a Kosmos.

As a young man he was priggish, snobby, scornful of "ordinary" people, snide, and very lonely. In letters from his teaching days in Long Island, he writes:

> I am getting to be a miserable kind of a dog;
> I am sick of wearing away by inches, and
> spending the fairest portion of my little span
> of life, here in this nest of bears, this forsaken
> of all Go[d]'s creation; among clowns and
> country bumpkins, fat-heads, and coarse
> brown-faced girls, dirty, ill-favored young
> brats, with squalling throats and crude man-
> ner, and bog-trotters, with all the disgust-
> ing conceit, of ignorance and vulgarity. . . .
> Never before have I entertained so low an
> idea of the beauty and perfection of man's
> nature, never have I seen humanity in so
> degraded a shape, as here.—Ignorance, vul-
> garity, rudeness, conceit, and dulness are the
> reigning gods of this deuced sink of despair.

Snide, and a little treacherous—these were people who had taken him into their community and
were paying him to be their children's teacher—
but, and this surely would come to save him, he
was lonely. Loneliness may be the most underestimated element in the shaping, reshaping, of character; it would be finally what drove Whitman to
New York, and to his almost compulsive cultiva-

tion and accumulation of friends and comrades. We don't know what particular events, or traumas, might have been the determinants in the glorious shift from the little prig in these letters, who disdains everyone and everything around him, who is almost the negative to the all-accepting, all-ennobling person of *Walt Whitman*, but surely at some point he would have realized that the bubble he had created around him not only insulated him but kept others from responding in any decent way to him. Response becomes in his poems the single most persistent theme: his passionately sympathetic response to the world around him, and his wish for sympathetic and sufficient return from the readers of his words. "*Respondez! Respondez!*" is how "Poem of the Propositions of Nakedness," from the 1856 edition, begins.

And thus he made himself, of such unlikely raw materials. But which of us isn't a similar jerry-built motion machine? Which of us doesn't sometimes feel that we're weird pop-ups of impulses, ambitions, desires, and dreams? But we don't live in poems, even those of us who are poets; unlike Whitman, we plunge into our poems, but then we emerge: we are the makers of our poems—Whitman's poems made him; he existed in them in a way he existed nowhere else. Even the person the rest of us engender to make our poems sometimes doesn't work very well; we can seem to chug along with a barely functioning engine. Who, poet or not, doesn't at times like that feel a tremulous doubt about the personage and life we've made up, from what we thought were our noblest impulses but which may actually have been glaring personal ineptitudes?

There are a few moments in his poems when Whitman doubts like that, darkly, deeply. In "Crossing Brooklyn Ferry," there's a confession almost frightening in its harrowing frankness, its self-downsizing, all in cadences that are all the more relentless in their echoes of his usual concussive confidence.

> It is not upon you alone the dark patches fall,
> The dark threw its patches down upon me also,
> The best I had done seem'd to me blank and
>   suspicious,
> My great thoughts as I supposed them, were
>   they not in reality meagre?
>
> Nor is it you alone who know what it is to be
>   evil,
> I am he who knew what it was to be evil,
> I too knotted the old knot of contrariety,
> Blabb'd, blush'd, resented, lied, stole, grudg'd,

Had guile, anger, lust, hot wishes I dared not
*   speak,*
Was wayward, vain, greedy, shallow, sly,
*   cowardly, malignant,*
The wolf, the snake, the hog, not wanting in
*   me,*
The cheating look, the frivolous word, the
*   adulterous wish, not wanting . . . .*

                                    (*LG*, 1856, 1860)

And again, in "As I Ebb'd with the Ocean of Life," the doubts are dire, and more directly about his poet-self.

O baffled, balk'd,
Bent to the very earth, here preceding what
*   follows,*
Oppressed with myself that I have dared to
*   open my mouth,*
Aware now, that amid all the blab whose
*   echoes recoil upon me, I have not once had*
*   the least idea who or what I am,*
But that before all my insolent poems the
*   real ME still stands untouched, untold,*
*   altogether unreached,*
Withdrawn far, mocking me with
*   mock-congratulary signs and blows,*

With peals of distant ironical laughter at every
*   word I have written or shall write,*
Striking me with insults until I fall helpless
*   upon the ground.*

                    (*LG*, 1860)

We could say that this is the standard poet's depression and fear of failure, what a friend—Paul Zweig, actually—once joked to me is "the common cold of the artistic personality." But Whitman doesn't doubt like this for very long, not the Whitman of the poems—that Whitman was a stunningly successful, hardly ever flagging poetical-fictional colossus. Driven by, transported by, exalted by his verse, he created themes and variations on every aspect of himself, real and unreal, factual and imagined, approved them, improved them. He could reveal the ill-wrought and the well-wrought of himself with equal fervor, and validate all of it with his singing, as he put it, his chant.

"*Who goes there!*" he asks, with exclamation point, "*. . . hankering, gross, mystical, nude?*" And compliments himself with no nod whatsoever to humility, not *that* kind, civil or social.

I do not snivel that snivel the world over,
That months are vacuums and the ground but
*   wallow and filth,*

> *That life is a suck and a sell, and nothing*
> *remains at the end but threadbare crape*
> *and tears.*

He says it, shouts it, then his music takes him into one of those delightfully delirious flights where he seems to lose track completely of anything like precise meaning.

> *Whimpering and truckling fold with powders*
> *for invalids . . . . conformity goes to the*
> *fourth removed,*
> *I cock my hat as I please indoors or out.*

What? " . . . truckling fold with powders . . . " What does that mean? It doesn't matter—he's singing himself, that's what we're meant to hear. Moments like this reinforce the sense of exuberance in the poetry. Not only is Whitman sensing and seeing with his gargantuan inclusive appetite, but at times he doesn't care at all if his assembling of sounds, his dance with his language leads to near incomprehensibility: he's like an abstract painter slashing his vowels and consonants across the auditory canvas in utter certainty that their effect won't be, can't be denied.

The civil, the social, the polite, forget all that. Forget chanting the erotic, which he does again and again. Forget the merely erotic, the sexually audacious:

> *Hair, bosom, hips, bend of legs, negligent*
>> *falling hands—all diffused . . . . mine too*
>> *diffused,*
> *Ebb stung by the flow, and flow stung by the*
>> *ebb . . . . loveflesh swelling and deliciously*
>> *aching,*
> *Limitless limpid jets of love hot and*
>> *enormous . . . . quivering jelly of love . . . .*
>> *white-blow and delirious juice,*
> *Bridegroom-night of love working surely and*
>> *softly into the prostrate dawn,*
> *Undulating into the willing and yielding day,*
> *Lost in the cleave of the clasping and*
>> *sweetfleshed day.*

Forget that, if that's possible, because beyond that pure evocation of the (nongender-specific) act of sex, who would have thought you might *masturbate* in your poem, and make it sound pertinent, morally crucial?

> *Is this then a touch? . . . . quivering me to a*
>> *new identity*
> *Flames and ether making a rush for my*
>> *veins . . .*

You villain touch! what are you doing? . . . .
  my breath is tight in its throat;
Unclench your floodgates! you are too much
  for me.
Blind loving wrestling touch! Sheathed hooded
  sharptoothed touch!
Did it make you ache so leaving me?

But, back in the poem, not even very far after that passage, Whitman can turn without any
compunction whatsoever to religion; he can elaborate on and absorb the human impulse toward
divinity-making, religion-making, ritual-making,
and declare—how could he dare?—those rituals
as sufficient to him, *useful* to him, to his fiction
which by that epoch of his evolving poem is his
reality as well.

I do not despise you priests;
My faith is the greatest of faiths and the least
  of faiths,
Enclosing all worship ancient and modern,
  and all between ancient and modern,
Believing I shall come again upon the earth
  after five thousand years,
Waiting response from oracles . . . . honoring
  the gods . . . . saluting the sun,

Making a fetish of the first rock or stump . . . .
powowing with sticks in the circle of obis,
Helping the lama or brahmin as he trims the
lamps of the idols . . .

Walking the teokallis, spotted with gore from
the stone and knife—beating the serpent-
skin drum;
Accepting the gospels, accepting him that was
crucified, knowing assuredly that he is
divine . . .

The Notebooks

▦ It's fascinating to leaf through the early volumes of the notebooks—so many hints, so many half-formed notions of what's to come; so many glimmers and fragments of beloved passages; so many intimations of the great self who'll finally inhabit the poetry.

He writes things like this: " 'Every accession of originality of thought,' says the author of *Statesmen of the Commonwealth of England* [John Forster], 'brings with it necessarily an accession of a certain originality of style.' " He copies this out, and surely takes it to heart, but, fine, what artist hasn't had, or borrowed, the same realization?

And what artist hasn't inflicted his or her self with an admonition like this: "Make no quotations, and no reference to any other writers.—Lumber the writing with nothing—and let it go as lightly as a bird flies in the air—or a fish swims in the sea. Be careful not to temper down too much."

All well and good, but how many poets have then exploded into a creative frenzy like the one that took Whitman? All through the notebooks, he learns, he struggles, he prepares, prepares for he probably has only the barest whisper of what. Here he is a painfully inept version of . . . so much.

> *I will not descend among*
> *professors and capitalists,*
> *and good society—I will*
> *turn up the ends of my*
> *trowsers up around my boots,*[*]
> *and my cuffs back from*
> *my wrists and go among* *with*
> *the simple drivers and*

[*] Eliot surely couldn't have been familiar with this when he wrote in "The Love Song of J. Alfred Prufrock," "I will wear the bottoms of my trousers rolled." How odd.

> *boatmen and men ~~who~~* *that*
> *catch fish or ~~hoe corn~~* *work in the field.*
> *I know ~~that~~ they are*
> *sublime*

He writes, he writes, he writes: note after note, many of which later will germinate into images and narratives, but still there is no conclusive evidence as to how the music finally started, how the poems, and the person in them, finally flourished in that music; no compelling deduction can be made at all from all of it. Something happened, some utterly mysterious thing happened in the psyche of the poet which still remains the unlikeliest miracle, and he discovered, created his method.

Here's an instance: he seems to be coming close to the poem, some of the material here will be lifted into it. He raggedly notes to himself: "For example, whisper privately in your ear . . . the studies . . . be a rich investment if they . . . to bring the hat instantly off the . . . all his learning and bond himself to feel and fully enjoy . . . superb wonder of a blade of grass growing up green and crispy from the ground. Enter into the thoughts of the different theological faiths—effuse all that the believing Egyptian would—all that the Greek—

all that the Hindoo, worshipping Brahma—the Koboo adoring his fetish stone or log."

Yet, how far, how far he still is, in poetic quality, even in conception, from the poems. In the notebook is written: "Superb wonder of a blade of grass growing up green and crispy from the ground." This is what it would evolve to:

> A child said, What is the grass? fetching it to
> me with full hands;
> How could I answer the child? . . . . I do not
> know what it is any more than he.
>
> I guess it must be the flag of my disposition,
> out of hopeful green stuff woven.
>
> Or I guess it is the handkerchief of the Lord,
> A scented gift and remembrancer designedly
> dropped,
> Bearing the owner's name someway in the
> corners, that we may see and remark and
> say Whose?

How far in time was that "green and crispy" from this? It may have been mere months, or weeks: however long it was, there's not enough duration to account for that amazingly sudden flare. Weeks? Years? He must have written the whole of the 1855 book in a matter of months; there doesn't seem to be any other space in his biography for it. Later, when he's planning the next and the next volume, he doesn't, as I noted, hesitate to project hundreds of poems over a short period. He must have felt his poetic energy was absolutely fluent and absolutely without limit. He could have planned *thousands* of poems, he was that charged with confidence, that certain of the force of his imagination and his music which he could roll out before himself like a wave whenever he wished.

Emerson and the Greatest Poet

Whitman was inconsistent about his possible debt to Emerson, especially to Emerson's famous essay "The Poet," which appeared in 1844. On several occasions he denied the influence of Emerson entirely; on the other hand, he once proclaimed: "I was simmering, simmering, simmering; Emerson brought me to a boil."* Emerson's essay does

---

* Emerson's now well-known reply to Whitman's having sent him the first *Leaves of Grass* was wholly gratifying to Whitman, more than he probably could have hoped for. "I am not blind to the worth of the wonderful gift of *Leaves of*

have a number of something like prescriptions for the large character and larger tasks of the poet he promulgates, some of which Whitman fulfilled, whether he had Emerson in mind or not. I find most intriguing though several comments Emerson makes on the possible form of poems, rather than his thematic suggestions. He writes, for instance: "It is not metres, but a metre-making argument that makes a poem,—a thought so passionate and alive, that, like the spirit of a plant or animal, it has an architecture of its own." A "metre-making argument" seems a useful way to characterize one of the routes Whitman found toward his music, and the poems themselves embody precisely that.

And later Emerson writes:

> The poet also resigns himself to his mood,
> and that thought which agitated him is

Grass," Emerson wrote, "I find it the most extraordinary piece of wit and wisdom that America has yet contributed. . . . I give you joy of your free and brave thought. I have joy in it. I find incomparable things said incomparably well, as they must be. . . . I greet you at the beginning of a great career, which yet must have had a long foreground somewhere, for such a start." Whitman printed the letter, without asking Emerson's permission, in the next, 1856 edition, and it began the downward spiral of their friendship. Emerson finally came to mistrust the poems, or at least their frankness about sex, and tried to convince Whitman to censor them.

expressed, but *alter idem*, in a manner totally new. The expression is organic, or, the new type which things themselves take when liberated. . . . Like the metamorphosis of things into higher organic forms, is their change into melodies. Over everything stands its daemon, or soul, and, as the form of the thing is reflected by the eye, so the soul of the thing is reflected by a melody. The sea, the mountain-ridge, Niagara, and every flowerbed, pre-exist, or super-exist, in pre-cantations, which sail like odors in the air.

Intriguing term, "pre-cantations." One more, perhaps even more germane: "The poet knows that he speaks adequately . . . only when he speaks somewhat wildly." Which certainly Whitman did: there had been no poem in literature before him that had anything approaching the wildness of Whitman's language and structure.

At any rate, whatever the debt Whitman directly may have owed to Emerson,[*] in his preface to the first *Leaves of Grass*, he takes Emerson's "poet" and

---

[*] It's even been suggested that Emerson also influenced Whitman's poetic cadences with his own prose—an interesting thought, though I can't see any real link.

enlarges him to what he calls "the Greatest Poet," offering a program similar to Emerson's, though on a scale that makes Emerson's seem timid. Whitman uses the "Greatest Poet" locution almost as a refrain in his preface, many of the thoughts of which he recasts, without the term "greatest," in the poem "By Blue Ontario's Shore."

In the preface, though, he implements the term "greatest poet" frankly, without qualms, without humility, but with no particular pride yet either: it's merely the way he characterizes his intentions. However, the qualities he gives to his imagined greatest poet, the methods he hypothesizes for him, and the character he demands of him, if they do echo Emerson a bit, aren't like anything in even the most fantastic primer for poets. Whitman denigrates technique for its own sake; he slights even extraordinary poetic genius. "The pleasure of poems is not in them that take the handsomest measure and similes and sound," he proclaims, and goes on: "Without effort and without exposing the least how it is done the greatest poets . . . ."

He begins his statement of intent—which is what the preface really is—by speaking of America, in a paragraph of strange, jagged diction, which sounds like the rebuttal to something that was just pronounced by an antagonist, a naysayer:

> America does not repel the past or what
> it has produced under its forms or amid
> other politics or the idea of castes or the
> old religions . . . . accepts the lesson with
> calmness . . . is not so impatient as has
> been supposed that the slough still sticks to
> opinions and matters and literature while
> the life which served its requirements has
> passed into the new life of the new forms . . .
> perceives that the corpse is slowly borne
> from the eating and sleeping rooms of
> the house . . . perceives that it waits a little
> while in the door . . . that it was fittest for
> its days . . . that its action has descended to
> the stalwart and wellshaped heir who ap-
> proaches . . . and that he shall be fittest for
> his days.

Then he postulates a clear absurdity, yet one that is essential to his argument: "The Americans of all nations at any time upon the earth have probably the fullest poetical nature. The United States themselves are essentially the greatest poem." His evidence for this, for the "genius" of the country, is in the way America is defined by "the common people," whose virtues he then summarizes in a passage of generalizations that foreshadow the particulars the poems will exalt. "Their manners speech dress friendships—the freshness and candor of their physiognomy—the picturesque looseness of their carriage . . . their deathless attachment to freedom." All winding down to a startling perception, "the terrible significance of their elections." "These too," he observes, "are unrhymed poetry. It awaits the gigantic and generous treatment worthy of it."

When he does get around to his greatest poet's aesthetic characteristics, when he begins to enumerate and define them, he sounds not so much like Emerson, but rather more like some perfectly sympathetic and brilliantly perspicacious commentator recounting the literary and moral virtues of the poems of *Leaves of Grass*. Anyone interested in Whitman should read the whole preface closely; its observations are often as inspired as in the poems, and it uses many of their methods. Here are a few of the greatest poet passages:

"He sees eternity less like a play with a prologue and denouement . . . . he sees eternity in men and women . . . . he does not see men and women as dreams or dots."

"Now he has passed that way see after him! there is not left any vestige of despair or misanthropy or cunning or exclusiveness or the ignominy of a nativity or color or delusion of hell or the necessity of hell . . . . and no man thenceforward shall be degraded for ignorance or weakness or sin."

"The greatest poet hardly knows pettiness or triviality. He is a seer . . . . he is individual . . . . he is complete in himself . . . . the others are as good as he, only he sees it and they do not."

"The greatest poet does not moralize or make applications of morals . . . . he knows the soul. The soul has that measureless pride which consists in never acknowledging any lessons but its own. But it has sympathy as measureless as its pride and the one balances the other and neither can stretch too far while in stretches in company with the other."

"The greatest poet has less a marked style and is more the channel of thoughts and things without increase or diminution, and is the free channel of himself. He swears to his art, I will not be meddlesome, I will not have in my writing any elegance or effect or originality to hang in the way between me and the rest like curtains."

It's especially interesting to note the way Whitman's exhortations for his character, his personality, his moral self, are fused here with his aspirations and ambitions for his work. That's always, for young artists, a quandary: basically, where do you start? When Machado speaks of the necessity of inventing a poet to compose a poem, the poet isn't a mere technician, isn't just an artist—the person who does the creation is a constant work in progress, perhaps finally realized through the poems themselves, but grounded in the difficult demands that all conscious humans must ask of themselves. Whitman asks a great deal and fulfills, at least in the person of the poem, nearly all.

The Greatest Poet Submits a Poem for Publication

. . . to Harpers magazine with what has to be the Greatest Accompanying Letter ever hazarded to an editor:

Is there any other poem of the sort extant— or indeed hitherto attempted?

You may start at the style. Yes, it is a new style, of course, but that is necessitated by new theories, new themes—or say the new treatment of themes, forced upon us for American purposes. Every really new person,

(poet or other,) makes his style—sometimes
a little way removed from the previous mod-
els—sometimes very far removed.

Furthermore I have surely attained
headway enough with the American public,
especially with the literary classes, to make it
worth your while to give them a sight of me
with all my neologism.

The price is $40. Cash down on
acceptance . . .

Should my name be printed in the pro-
gramme of contributors at any time it must
not be lower down than third in the list.

If the piece is declined, please keep the MS.
for me to be called for. Will send, or call, last
of next week.

Walt Whitman

Harpers rejected the poem.

"I"

Archilochos begins it, in the seventh century
B.C., this odd, unreasonable, unjustifiable tradition of the poet speaking of him or herself, as
though what happened to the poet, what he or

she did, felt, thought, might matter to anyone
else.

> *My ash spear is my barley bread,*
> *My ash spear is my Ismarian wine.*
> *I lean on my spear and drink.*

Says Archilochos, translated, channeled really,
by Guy Davenport: "*I lean on my spear and drink.*"
And Whitman in the second stanza of his *Leaves*
says:

> *I loafe and invite my soul,*
> *I lean and loaf at my ease . . . . observing a*
> *   spear of summer grass.*

And who cares about either in their hanging
around?

The opening of the original "Song of Myself"
has been taken as an establishing of a metaphysical stance, a sociopolitical identification, the proclamation of a new vision of culture and art. And,
truly, it's all of these things, and more. But it is also,
in some ways most important, a reaffirmation of
the lyric "I," a taking it back to its original audacity, its response to that absurd question of why,
when Homer's epics already exist with their cast
of thousands, their battles, their emotional con-
frontations, their mass of history, anyone should

bother to listen when this single sung voice, this Archilochos, this Sappho, moans of love, or war, or anger, or . . . *leaning, loafing, drinking.*

Why should it be that this enormous faculty humans possess, imagination, would be put to the use of embodying, enacting, singing, a single soul, rather than a nation's, an epoch's, a civilization's?

> *The atmosphere is not a perfume . . . it has no*
> *taste of the distillation . . . it is odorless,*
> *It is for my mouth forever . . . . I am in love*
> *with it,*
> *I will go to the bank by the wood and become*
> *undisguised and naked,*
> *I am mad for it to be in contact with me.*

"*Undisguised and naked.*" That was what Archilochos was as he presented himself, celebrated himself, as soldier, mercenary, sometimes even as coward; as lover, as whore-monger, sometimes whipped dog, groveller, bearer of unredeemed resentment, but, most important, as "*I,*" and sometimes addressing another single person: a "*you.*"

"*You are too old for perfume,*" Archilochos says to some sad woman as he rejects her, some forlorn, utterly unknown, utterly forgotten woman who still exists, still exists, in her tiny fragment of what was probably a tiny poem. And,

> *Houses and rooms are full of perfumes . . . .*
> *the shelves are crowded with perfumes . . .*

writes Whitman, as though he heard Archilochos again, and reenacts again the meager single, intellectually ungrounded self again: "*I breathe the fragrance myself, and know it and like it.*"

What does the *intellect* have to do with any of this? How can mind sanction such a preposterous act of self-aggrandizement; call it egotism, narcissism, call it what you like, it's ridiculous. With that insignificant "I," introduced into the packet of Archilochos's poems, that strange phenomenon of language heightened to music, civilization changes, all human life changes: the person changes, perhaps the "person" in fact is brought into being—perhaps before that poetic "I" only kings and queens and war- or athletic-heroes had real persons. Might it finally have been the poets who gave the lover his or her "I"; the peasant, the ordinary soldier, the ordinary blacksmith, ordinary wife, adulterer, adulteress, each his or her "I"?

And might Whitman have been trying, in the largest sense (and the smallest), to revivify that lyric "I," to enlarge it, to make it grand again, make it more audacious, more authentic than ever by giving it the entire universe, physical and spiritual, as its domain? *"I am mad for it to be in contact with me."* Mad for it, mad for myself: "The Song of Myself" isn't even called that in the first edition, it would only be titled later, but it had to be there all along: Song of Myself, song of me, of me as you, song of me as everyone, and Whitman means it: *everyone.*

In the original preface he goes on at length about "democracy," and "America," claiming for his poems a unifying, generating purpose somehow related to them, and he'll return to the theme throughout his life. But his preface moves quickly off to more general considerations of the ends he'll attempt: "The soul has that measureless pride which consists in never acknowledging any lessons but its own. But it has sympathy as measureless as its pride, and the one balances the other and neither can stretch too far while it stretches in company with the other."

This is the particular secret with which Whitman will inform his "I"—its sympathy. He is going to create a self that will be "I" in a way no one else had ever done it, not in lyric poetry anyway; the container and enactor and, he hopes, the redeemer of others' "I"s, others' selves, others' un-acknowledged selves: really he wants to offer the lyric "I" to us all.

> For every atom belonging to me as good
>> belongs to you.

He doesn't mean that we inevitably share the atoms of the universe, as Democritus and then the science of Whitman's time had recently proposed; he means rather that we share the atoms of ourselves, the smallest particles of what makes up our experience, our souls: he means that if we follow him, listen to him, maybe sing with him, we can be the poet of ourselves. And as Archilochos absurdly asked us to listen to his plaints and plights, and meant it, Whitman means this, too.

> These are the thoughts of all men in all ages
>> and lands, they are not original with me,
> If they are not yours as much as mine they are
>> nothing or next to nothing,
> If they do not enclose everything they are next
>> to nothing,
> If they are not the riddle and the untying of
>> the riddle they are nothing,
> If they are not just as close as they are distant
>> they are nothing.

A Dare

◈ And yet "I celebrate myself" has to be seen as more than a conventional prelude to a lyrical aesthetic event: it is a proclamation of poetic independence and uniqueness.

"And what I assume you shall assume" is a confrontation, really a challenge, a dare: what is being implied here is that the ordinary relationship between reader and poet, lyrical speaker, lyrical "I," will not be in effect. Something else is happening, something which, on the face of it, is presumptuous. An impertinence which is absurdly reinforced by the notification of a communion unlike any other in poetry: you are not merely listening to me, overhearing me—you are to be taken into my poem with me in a way no other poem has done it.

And furthermore—"For every atom belonging to me as good belongs to you"—not only are we not to be in a conventional poet–reader relation, we will be in a conceptually unheard of physical, then metaphysical (because we are dissolved beyond our elementary material identity into one another) connectedness. And, the poem goes on, now that our unique aesthetic affiliation has been established, we'll relax for a moment into a traditional lyrical-pastoral situation, this time with the reader dismissed for a moment from the concussion of our initial coming together. "I," just "I" alone, will repose now—"I loaf and invite my soul"—and allow you to consider for a few phrases what has just passed between us. I'll look around for a moment, while you observe me in the way you have always observed the poet in his poem.

But the poem will go on to establish in the next stanzas that there is, as seemed to be indicated, an "I" unlike any other that has ever existed in a poem; it is an identity that is at once intensely, almost overwhelmingly, sensual, and self-consciously prophetic. Compared to this, even the personage Dante created for his poetic universe remains resolutely unpretentious: he is always Dante, the sensing, thinking, swooning maker of his verses, who trembles before the magnitude of the spiritual matters he confronts. He inhabits, in another words, the same poetic self as did Archilochos when he first devised the marvel of the "I" of a poem.

Whitman wants to surpass this. He is not only going to make a poem for us, but he is going to take us to the very *source* of poems, the mine from which poetry is tunneled out.

Have you practiced so long to learn to read?
Have you felt so proud to get at the meaning
*   of poems?*

Stop this day and night with me and you shall
*   possess the origin of all poems,*
You shall possess the good of the earth and
*   sun . . . . there are millions of suns left,*
You shall no longer take things at second or
*   third hand . . . . nor look through*
the eyes of the dead . . . . nor feed on the
*   spectres in books,*
You shall not look through my eyes, nor take
*   things from me, you shall listen to all sides*
*   and filter them from yourself.*

The promise, the promise in much of the work, is that the vividness and grandeur of the poetic self who is making this poem will be so gravitationally magnetic that he will make poets of us all; we will not only be accounted for, we will learn to account for ourselves, and for everything else. We will be again first persons adequate to our greatest selves.

"You"

▦ What a confusing, intriguing, inspiring, finally marvelous jumble of second persons!

Four pages into the song, which has mostly been knittings and hammerings about "I," with its first "you"s, mostly indicating the reader, the experiencer of the poem, suddenly a quite different addressee:

> *I believe in you my soul . . . . the other I am*
> *must not abase itself to you,*
> *And you must not be abased to the other.*

All right, a traditional address of self to soul, though perhaps a bit more complex, because of that third-person "other," which implies a splitting of the "I" speaking to the "you." But now:

> *Loafe with me on the grass . . . . loose the stop*
> *from your throat,*
> *Not words, not music or rhyme I want . . . .*
> *not custom or lecture, not even the best,*
> *Only the lull I like, the hum of your valved*
> *voice.*

A bit of ambiguity here. Grammatically, the addressee would be the immediate antecedent, which implies the soul, the soul distinct from the other in the self, who might be less, but mustn't be admitted really to be such. But can "you" be the reader as well? Not likely: the reader's "valved voice" can't be part of the proceedings. It has still to be the second person of the self that's being addressed, the part of poet which is distinct from self, who has purified his intentions so much that there is not only not custom, nor lecture, just the lull, the hum of the voice, valved like a musical instrument.

> *I mind how we lay in June, such a transparent*
> *summer morning;*
> *You settled your head athwart my hips and*
> *gently turned over on me,*
> *And parted the shirt from my bosom-bone,*
> *and plunged your tongue to my barestript*
> *heart,*
> *And reached till you felt my beard, and*
> *reached till you held my feet.*

But what possible antecedent is here in this erotically charged disrobing (very notorious now, taken as the first evidence in the poems of Whitman's homosexuality)? A lover of some sort, or is again it a personified soul? What happens is that both possibilities resonate together, reinforcing each other: there is a self, there is an other, there is an act so intense it can only be embodied in something like sex, and there is, still, the "you" of the self, all in harmony together like the strings of a musical instrument.

And the way the poem moves over the next stanza break (stanza breaks in Whitman mean something different from what they previously had; they presage the leapings about of Surrealism and its half-delirious offshoots) as we cross the banks of this stanza and head into the next, we bring the fusions of the previous one with us, but go on into another condition of thought and emotion entirely: we arrive at the numinous, the language of the holy.

> *Swiftly arose and spread around me the peace*
> *   and joy and knowledge that pass all the art*
> *   and argument of the earth . . .*

Bliss! A bliss beyond the erotic. Which, through its redescent into the world of seemingly trivial things—leaves, ants, moss, and the rest—is transfigured to an awareness unlike what might be expected from the most ecstatic sexual union.

> *And I know that the hand of God is the*
> *   elderhand of my own,*

> *And I know that the spirit of God is the eldest*
> > *brother of my own,*
> *And that all the men ever born are also my*
> > *brothers . . . . and the women my sisters*
> > *and lovers,*
> *And that a kelson of the creation is love;*
> *And limitless are leaves stiff or drooping in the*
> > *fields,*
> *And brown ants in the little wells beneath*
> > *them,*
> *And mossy scabs of the wormfence, and*
> > *heaped stones, and elder and mullen and*
> > *pokeweed.*

Where are we? Where have we been? Who is "we"? The "you" who was Whitman's soul, and the "you" whose voice was lulling, and the "you" who was sexually united with the speaker, have become like protoplasm, shape-shifting, identity-shifting, transformed even to something that unifies with divinity, then, as the poem goes on, with humanity, all of it, and creation, and love, and then nature, even to the ants, even to scabs of moss, and stones, and the lowest of the weeds.

The relationship of the poet, the voice of the poet, to "you" continues to evolve throughout "Song of Myself." Finally what is arrived at is a pedagogical relation; the reader becomes a kind of apprentice to the poet—we're being instructed on arriving at a condition of consciousness like the one the poem demonstrates and proposes.

> *Long enough have you dreamed contemptible*
> *   dreams,*
> *Now I wash the gum from your eyes,*
> *You must habit yourself to the dazzle of the*
> *   light and of every moment of your life . . .*

The poem tells us, and:

> *I teach straying from me, yet who can stray*
> *   from me?*
> *I follow you whoever you are from the present*
> *   hour;*
> *My words itch at your ears till you understand*
> *   them.*

And even goes so far as to tell us that we have been colonized by the voice of the poem and will be carried along by it, like it or not.

> *I do not say these things for a dollar, or to fill*
> *   up the time while I wait for a boat;*
> *It is you talking just as much as myself . . . . I*
> *   act as the tongue of you,*

> *It was tied in your mouth . . . . in mine it*
> > *begins to be loosened.*

Still, like all great teachers, the poem-poet tells us of its own limits, and of our own responsibilities as neophytes.

> *Not I, not any one else can travel that road*
> > *for you,*
> *You must travel it yourself . . .*

It's so exhilarating to travel those sidereal ways and byways with Whitman. In a poem from 1856, "To You," a somewhat lesser statement of the theme, he enlarges on the specific redemptive notions of his third-person address, making certain that no possible "you," however imperfect, however depressed, will be omitted.

> *The mockeries are not you,*
> *Underneath them and within them I see you*
> > *lurk,*
> *I pursue you where none else has pursued you,*
> *Silence, the desk, the flippant expression,*
> > *the night, the accustom'd routine, if these*
> > *conceal you from others or from yourself,*
> > *they do not conceal you from me,*
> *The shaved face, the unsteady eye, the impure*

> *complexion, if these balk others they do not*
>   *balk me,*
> *The pert apparel, the deform'd attitude,*
>   *drunkenness, greed, premature death, all*
>   *these I part aside.*

In the "Song," though, the enlarging is perhaps even more radical: by the end of the poem, the "you" being addressed—is it the reader bent over the page, or might it in fact be enlarged to be God himself?

> *Listener up there! Here you . . . . what have*
>   *you to confide to me?*
> *Look in my face while I snuff the sidle of*
>   *evening,*
> *Talk honestly, for no one else hears you, and I*
>   *stay only a minute longer.*

Then, that famous challenge:

> *Do I contradict myself?*
> *Very well then . . . . I contradict myself;*
> *I am large . . . . I contain multitudes.*

And again, a different sort of dare, of effrontery:

> *Will you speak before I am gone? Will you*
>   *prove already too late?*

Then comes a sudden socketing back in the world, a world which in Whitman's cosmology now has been incorporated, infused, enlarged; in gorgeous and utterly unlikely language.

> *The spotted hawk swoops by and accuses*
>   *me . . . . he complains of my gab and my*
>   *loitering.*

("My gab and my loitering." Who else could conjoin those utterly ordinary words and make them resonate so?)

Then the gloriously audacious utterance:

> *I too am not a bit tamed . . . . I too am*
>   *untranslatable,*
> *I sound my barbaric yawp over the roofs of*
>   *the world.*

The poem could well stop there, but it doesn't want to leave without us, in our new form as exalted, unified, comprehensive and comprehending second person.

> *I bequeath myself to the dirt to grow from the*
>   *grass I love,*
> *If you want me again look for me under your*
>   *bootsoles.*

You will hardly know who I am or what I
    mean,
But I shall be good health to you nonetheless,
And filter and fibre your blood.

Failing to fetch me at first keep encouraged,
Missing me one place search another,
I stop some where waiting for you.

How crucially appropriate it is that the last word of the "Song" is "you."

America

How he loves America in that first preface to *Leaves of Grass*. Like a schoolboy, like a youth in an unquestioning patriotic frenzy. How ragingly later on, before and during the Civil War, he would curse the "disunionists" who dared sunder the nation, sunder his hopes for its greatness. And how he loves democracy. The vision he has for democracy, his hopes for America, are almost painful to bring to mind. How short we have fallen compared to what he saw for us, how in so many ways have we regressed.

Whitman wants his poem to be democracy embodied, enacted; he wants to omit nothing.

Democracy at its essence is the detail, not the generalization, or at least the detail first, then the generalization; the "I," because we have to begin there, and the "we," and then the "you," and there, in essence, the equation is done—there is, as he points out again and again, no "they": "they" is the thought of the crowd, the mob, the mockers. Even during the Civil War, however nearly obsessed he was about preserving the Union, the being-together, the Confederate warriors are still a portion of "we," his compassion never flags, no matter who is firing the weapon, who receiving the wound.

He really meant all that rhetoric in the first preface; he really did want his poetry to help, or compel what he thought America could be, had to be. He really believed his poetry was an efficient implement for creating the America of his vision. Although first he wanted to enable Americans to be sufficient to that nation—he believed his words would signify and seduce them from their incomplete awareness of the task—Americans who would then construct the America he knew was latent, and necessary, for the country's future. He happily confounds (and only in retrospect absurdly conflates) the future of the country with his vision of the poet who will embody it.

"Of all nations the United States with veins full of poetical stuff most need poets and will doubtless have the greatest and use them the greatest. Their Presidents shall not be their common referee so much as their poets shall."

Later, after he's written the great poems, he states, in *Democratic Vistas*, just as passionately the connection he believes there must exist between his work and his country's destiny:

> I say no land or people or circumstances
> ever existed so needing a race of singers
> and poems differing from all others, and
> rigidly their own, as the land and people
> and circumstances of our United States
> need such singers and poems today, and
> for the future. . . . As long as the States
> continue to absorb and be dominated by
> the poetry of the Old World, and remain
> unsupplied with autochthonous song, to
> express, vitalize and give color to and de-
> fine their material and political success, and
> minister to them distinctively, so long will
> they stop short of first-class Nationality and
> remain defective.

His hopes for us were limitless; he even pos-
tulated, in the poems and in *Democratic Vistas*, a

certain physique for the American, a certain degree of health. He often, too often perhaps, speaks of "health," in various manifestations; he loves the word itself and finds dozens of ways of indicating it in the body and mind, and even in institutions: "These American states strong and healthy and accomplished shall receive no pleasure from violations of natural models." (Sad, considering how young he was when his own body began to turn against him with a series of strokes, the first at the terribly early age of fifty-four, then later, in the various disabilities of aging.)

Interestingly, he's aesthetically very conscious, cunning, about the best way to embody his patriotism. In the first edition of *Leaves*, after going on such at great length about America in the preface, he's a good long way into the poem before the word ever appears, and it does so then in the introduction of the author I quoted before: "Walt Whitman, an American, one of the roughs, a kosmos." And further, though he invokes the battle of Goliad in the Mexican War; then a famous American sea battle, and the names of several states and cities (including Montreal), the word never again appears in that first version of the poem. Not until the 1860 edition does the word make its rather theatrical appearance in "I Hear

America Singing," which, with its compilation of a long list of hardworking tradesmen and honest mothers and wives, sounds now like the progenitor of a hundred Broadway and Hollywood faux-proletariat musicals.

His not using the word "America," though, is more effective than not and honors his task more clearly: rather than refer directly to America, he makes his poem embody the nation at its best. He aestheticizes and spiritualizes America and its people; and he tells what a fully conscious American would see and feel if he could share Whitman's genius, and the poem does, of course, allow us to partake of that genius. The hundreds of American characters who populate and ennoble the poem, the dozens of anecdotes of their strength, their integrity, their distinctness—even when they lag, when they're part of a crowd, for instance, who are ridiculing a prostitute—he appeals to their native goodness, their compassion, their sympathy—*"Miserable! I do not laugh at your oaths or jeer you."*

Still, Whitman was no dreamer, no rose-lensed optimist, no self-deluder: he proves himself in the prose painfully aware of America's greater faults, its incompleteness, its derelictions, its corruptions and crassness and despicable failures.

In *Democratic Vistas*, he all but rants, as though tragically disappointed in his country: "Never was there, perhaps, more hollowness at heart than at present, and here in the United States . . . . What penetrating eye does not everywhere see through the mask? . . . We live in an atmosphere of hypocrisy throughout . . . . The depravity of the business classes of our country is not less than has been supposed, but infinitely greater. The official services of the America, national, state, and a municipal, in all their branches and departments, except the judiciary, are saturated in corruption, bribery, falsehood, mal-administrating; and the judiciary is tainted." He quotes a "foreigner," who reports similar gloomy observations, including one that strikes sadly home these days: "I have noticed more and more, the alarming spectacle of parties usurping the government, and openly and shamelessly wielding it for party purposes." (What we've come to now, politics by party, politics as power—doesn't that instruct us to mistrust, to loathe?) He already knew the loss, and almost with a cry against himself, though in his fervor of exaggeration he surely doesn't mean it, he laments, "America has yet morally and artistically originated nothing."

But of course it had, it had originated much, including *Leaves of Grass*, which is a hymn of praise to the nation, to its people, its land, its nature, its animals—*"When the mockingbird sounds his delicious gurgles, and cakes, and screams and weeps"*—and its cities, its rivers, and its *"gneiss and coal and long-threaded moss and fruits and grains and esculent roots."* Even the lowest, the slaves, and slavery, which in the preface he castigates: "Slavery and the tremulous spreading of hands to protect it, and the stern opposition to it which shall never cease till it ceases or the speaking of tongues and the moving of lips cease." And in the poems, again and again he powerfully and poignantly castigates it:

> *I am the hounded slave . . . . I wince at the*
>   *bite of the dogs,*
> *Hell and despair are upon me . . . . crack and*
>   *again crack the marksmen,*
> *I clutch the rails of the fence . . . . my gore*
>   *dribs thinned with the ooze of my skin,*
> *I fall on the weeds and stones,*
> *The riders spur their unwilling horses and*
>   *haul close,*
> *They taunt my dizzy ears . . . . they beat*
>   *me violently over the head with their*
>   *whip-stocks.*

And even again, his body, which is an American body, a body born of all his accumulations, all his accountings for, and which is composed in his ecstatic vision of all the other bodies, and even of those bodies dying and already in death: Americans, America, all of it. And the soul, the spirit, all of it, even those who have lost faith in the soul and spirit:

> Down-hearted doubters, dull and excluded,
> Frivolous sullen moping angry affected
> disheartened atheistial,
> I know every one of you, and I know the
> unspoken interrogatories.
> By experience I know them.

Then, immediately from that, one of his wild poetic somersaults:

> How the flukes splash!
> How they contort rapid as lightning, with
> spasms and spouts of blood!

A symbolization that he resolves as only he can:

> Be at peace bloody flukes of doubters and
> sullen mopers,
> I take my place among you as much as among
> any . . .

And so his vision not only encompasses the enemy soldier, the fireman, the slave, the adulteress, it includes the thrush and ant and weed: it's not incidental that he reaches back to the year one, "sesquillions" of cycles behind us—democracy includes past and future because its vision generates both, in a way even religion is unable to, or dares not to.

> *Cycles ferried my cradle, rowing and rowing*
> *   like cheerful boatmen;*
> *For room to me stars kept aside in their own*
> *   rings,*
> *They sent influences to look after what was to*
> *   hold me.*

Even when he addresses the universe itself, and the metaphysical universe he devolves from it, though he never has to say so overtly, he is still American, still firmly committed to the perspective, the viewing place the rest of the poem has created to contain him; no matter how far into eternity he reaches, he is there in his language, his beloved American language, which, in this early manifestation of it, he never for an instant betrays, as he will sometimes later, with what at better moments he'd called "European" poeticisms, contractions, artifices. (In "An American Primer," a sketch he wrote but never published, he proclaims it even more insistently: "I think I am done with many of the words of the past hundred centuries.—I am mad that their poems, bibles, word, still rule and represent the earth, and are not yet superseded.") In the poems themselves, no matter how elevated his theme, how grand his physics and metaphysics, his language insisted on being that of actual Americans, of the streets they inhabited, the cities and landscapes he believed made them great.

The Modern, One: Baudelaire

It's become almost reflexive in American poetry commentary to pair Whitman with his great contemporary Emily Dickinson, as though they were the two progenitors of modern American poetry. I admire Dickinson enormously, she was surely one of the greatest and one of the most intellectually keen poets who ever lived, but I don't believe that she's had, or at least not until fairly recently, anything like the influence she's reputed to on other poets—her aesthetic is too singular, too idiosyncratic, too personal to have anything like the cultural force Whitman's has had.

If there's any poet with whom I would pair Whitman, it would be Baudelaire: both of them redefined the elemental project of poetry, and both, to a great extent, indicated the direction, the opportunities, and the parameters of what we now call the modern.

The similarities between them are striking: they were born two years apart and incredibly enough were doing their best work during precisely the same period, publishing their seminal books within two years of each other, *Leaves of Grass* in 1855, *Les Fleurs du Mal* in 1857. Both books were prosecuted as obscene—Baudelaire's before it was even published, Whitman's later on, when the prudes realized what a revolutionary sensual threat his works effected.

Even in their private lives there are notable likenesses: both were especially conscious of their costume. Baudelaire was a self-proclaimed dandy and spent on clothes a good portion of the inheritance he was busily and finally tragically squandering. Whitman reflected at length on his appearance, arriving at a guise that was a mix of New York working man, "rough," a "b'hoy," one of the self-conscious urban wild men: in the famous frontispiece of the 1855 book he slouches with shirt collar casually opened, loose trousers, soft hat. In earlier photos he attempted a much more elegant style, with a dashing bow tie, tilted black fedora, trimmed beard and hair, decorative walking stick. (Sad premonition of the physical debilities that would afflict him so early in his life.)

Both were prowlers of the city. Both their cities were rapidly changing: Whitman's New York by its explosive growth as a port and commercial center; Paris as a result of the way Baron Haussmann, the powerful city planner, was wiping out so much of the history embedded in its ancient hives of houses.

La forme d'un ville
change plus vite, hélas! que le coeur d'un mortel

(Cities change so quickly, alas,
A mortal heart can't keep up)

Walter Benjamin in discussing Baudelaire and his city wrote, "Baudelaire loved solitude, but he wanted it in a crowd," and then described crowds, "in which no one is either quite transparent or quite opaque to all others."* What better description of Whitman in his urban wanderings?

---

* Marx also has something to say about poets that might describe both poets: "The poet enjoys the incomparable privilege of being himself and someone else as he sees fit. Like a roving soul in search of a body, he enters another person whenever he wishes. For him alone, all is open; if certain places seem closed to him, it is because in his view they are not worth inspecting."

But both poets were also compulsively gregarious. Both were magpies, gathering images, impressions, sounds, and dramas from the streets and from the hidden places behind city facades. Both, most important, were exalters, of the ordinary, the common and uncommon, the beautiful and seemingly repulsive. Baudelaire says: "The task was . . . to extract beauty from *Evil*." Whitman says, enlarging the thought, as though almost in response: "Folks expect of the poet to indicate more than the beauty and dignity which always attach to dumb real objects. . . . They expect him to indicate the path between reality and their souls."

Both were fascinated by, and wanted in their work and their visions to redeem, the real existence of the outcast and despised, the neglected and damned; which meant in fact *everyone*. Both in their way redefine artistic redemption. Here is Baudelaire on a woman "of a lower order":

> *Blanche fille aux cheveux roux,*
> *Dont la robe par ses trous*
> *Laisse voir la pauvreté*
>   *Et la beauté,*
>
> *Pour moi, poëte chétif,*
> *Ton jeune corps maladif,*

Plein de tache de rousseur,
      A sa douceur.

(White skinned red-haired girl,
through the holes in your dress,
peep poverty,
      and beauty.

For a puny poet like me,
your stricken young body,
splotched from head to feet—
      is still sweet.)

And here is Whitman:

The prostitute draggles her shawl, her bonnet
      bobs on her tipsy and pimpled neck,
The crowd laugh at her blackguard oaths, the
      men jeer and wink to each other . . .

They were profoundly similar in other ways as well. Baudelaire was trying, if never quite saying so, to complete the social and historical projects of the 1789 and 1848 revolutions, and to find the place that "evil"—which means ordinariness, ugliness, nonbeauty—would have to have in a post-revolutionary conscience. But more crucially for the eras that followed him, he was also investigating and embodying the unpredictability of the irrational, the inadmissables of the unconscious, while at the same time striving to preserve and perfect the aesthetic necessities of form, order, structure.

Whitman was supremely aware of the implications of the American Revolution, with its implicit promises of equality and equity; it was the place where he believed even his most personal spiritual ambitions had its origins. But his vision required him, like Baudelaire, to find new routes through the deterministic logics of mind and self that had come before him.

Both revolutionize poetry. Baudelaire: the master of existing forms, shaping the turmoil and social decadence he saw around him into the most exquisite, elegant, morally voracious verse. His perceptions appear to be in conflict with his revolutionary aspiration, but really aren't: his forms reach back, recuperate, rejuvenate, dilate the turmoil of the modern world with the tragic gaieties of traditional artistic mastery.

Whitman—though he didn't at first see himself that way—destroyer of form, creator of something entirely new, not only like Baudelaire in its matter, but in its utterance, its very shape: he created a new form to enact and encompass the world as he passionately wished it to be.

◈ Baudelaire, to his chagrin and perhaps as a factor in his ultimate self-destruction, had to contend with Victor Hugo: poet, novelist, essayist, polemicist of unreal energy and fluency; precocious inductee into the Academy; then active and successful politician; literally the most famous man in the world, with his own admirable social and political projects, his own vast ego, his domination of poetry and culture.

Baudelaire secretly despised Hugo but dedicated poem after poem to him. Hugo praised Baudelaire—"Your fleurs du mal shine and dazzle like stars . . . . I applaud your vigorous spirit with all my might"—but surely underestimated the significance of Baudelaire's work and never in his dreams would have imagined that for the future Baudelaire would define the aesthetics of the century that followed him, and that he, Hugo, as an influence, as a genius, would become more an item of nostalgia than a symbol of artistic power and significance.

Whitman didn't have to measure himself against Hugo, thank goodness, though he had to be aware of Hugo's astounding fame and influence; late in life he became in some ways his own Hugo, imagining himself (and to at least some degree really being) that crucial to his culture and society, that famous, that influential. All along, though, Whitman did have Longfellow.* Longfellow was terribly famous, and Whitman was painfully conscious of the other poet's commercial success. *The Song of Hiawatha* and the first edition of *Leaves of Grass* were published in the same year; *Hiawatha* in the ensuing twelve months sold thirty thousand copies; *Leaves of Grass*, a few hundred.

Perhaps even more rankling, Whitman's darling mother and his brother George "leafed through *Hiawatha* and the 1855 *Leaves of Grass* and, in George's words, 'the one seemed to us pretty much the same muddle as the other.'" It sounds like an unfunny Jewish-mother joke.

Later in his life Whitman found a place in his poetic universe for Longfellow, praising the other poet to his own circle of acolytes as an admirable example of the "European tradition." In a conversation, though, with his young friend Horace

---

* I should probably mention that I had Longfellow, too. He was my father's favorite poet, and my father would recite his poems to me, and even coax me into memorizing some. "Between the dark and the daylight, / when the night is beginning to lower, / comes a pause in the days occupation / that is known as the children's hour." My goodness, it's still there.

Traubel, who recorded literally volumes of his conversations with Whitman,[*] he said of Longfellow that he "never traveled new paths: of course never broke new paths: in fact was a man who shrank from unusual things—from what was highly colored, dynamic, drastic."[†]

In the end of course, just as Baudelaire has usurped what Hugo would surely have assumed was his place in posterity, Longfellow would have been thunderstruck to find his work all but forgotten, except as children's poetry, and to behold

---

[*] There's a useful selection, *Intimate with Walt,* edited by Gary Schmidgall, (Iowa City: University of Iowa Press, 2001).

[†] Still, there are some echoes of Longfellow in Whitman's poems. Longfellow begins *Evangeline*:

> *This is the forest primeval . . .*

And Whitman, (in "Pioneers! O Pioneers!" from 1865; one of his weakest poems), perhaps meaning to tear those forests, and Longfellow with them, down, writes: "We primeval forests felling . . . ." And later on in the same poem:

> *These are of us, they are with us,*
> *All for primal needed work . . .*

which has an uncomfortable metrical echo of the relentless pulse of "Hiawatha."

> *By the shores of Gitche Gumee,*
> *By the shining Big-Sea-Water . . .*

And in another poem: "I sing the password primeval." The same inversion as Longfellow's famous forest. Is this a little private joke? The odd locution seems beyond coincidental.

Whitman as the representative American poet to the readers and writers not only of his own country but of the world.

The Modern, Two: Eliot and Pound

▨ Eliot could be such a snob, and—one hopes unconsciously—a liar. Here he is early on in his career pontificating about Whitman: "Now, eccentricity of manner, however unavoidable, is apt to indicate that art has strayed dangerously far from its vital origin. Oddity is no part of solid artistic development; however beautiful or impressive, it is rather an excrescent outgrowth, bound to prove abortive, and at the same time to sap life from a parent stock which without it might grow more loftily and strongly. Walt Whitman's style is of this excrescent, abortive kind."

The truth is that despite his bloviating, the very essence of Eliot's poetical method is based on Whitman's. Eliot had a great, original ear and would surely have composed significant poetry without Whitman's influence, but Whitman's development of free verse surely offered Eliot a much wider-ranging voice than he could have had without it. Furthermore, Eliot's principal structural method, of thematic disconnectedness, the lyric accumulation of unpredictable and apparently unrelated poetic events—images, metaphors, varying voices—isn't to my mind evident anywhere before Whitman. Though Eliot preferred to cite the metaphysical English poets and the French symbolists as his principal influences (despite leaving out Baudelaire, who certainly had a profound effect on him), the way he actually put together his poems is found in none of them but is effectively realized in Whitman.

We have to remember how close in time Eliot was to Whitman—when Eliot was born, in 1881, Whitman was still alive and his fame was growing—and how much of a weight it must have been for Eliot when he was trying to establish his own poetic identity to have Whitman looming just behind him; what a pressing Oedipal temptation it would have been to denigrate him, and what obvious grounds for fibbing about your debts to him. The moral and philosophic similarities of the two poets are few—in character they're very different, and so are their poems— but it wasn't merely in structure that Whitman was a model for Eliot: Eliot's poetry in its scope and grand intentions surely owes much to Whitman's example.* Still, what's most crucial for Eliot was Whitman's discovery of a way to structure a poem that gave his work so much flexibility and range and allowed him to move effortlessly and with forceful effect from the detail to the metaphysical, and which offered Eliot, too, a way to expand his poetic speculations.†

* Even the title of Eliot's first successful poem, "The Love Song of J. Alfred Prufrock," echoes Whitman's title "Song of Myself." In a poem colored by extreme irony, this seems quite likely to have been intentional. And beyond the title, though the moods of the two poems couldn't be less alike, there are some odd similarities between them. For example, just as Whitman's "Song" begins with an "I" inviting a "you" into its presence, so Eliot's begins:

> Let us go then, you and I,
> When the evening is spread out against the sky
> Like a patient etherized upon a table . . .

† I can't resist comparing a well-known passage from "Four Quartets," a quotation from Julian of Norwich, one of Eliot's esoteric Christian sources, to a passage of Whitman's. Eliot, in Julian's voice, solemnly intones:

> All shall be well, and
> All manner of things shall be well . . .

But here is that old "excrescent" Whitman in "To Think of Time":

> What will be will be well—for what is well,
> To take interest is well, and not to take interest shall be
>   well.

Eliot himself of course was a profoundly liberating influence on other poets, including among many others Ezra Pound, who was both his master and his student. Pound is often deemed the great modernist innovator, but his own poetry didn't attain its fullest form, in the *Cantos*, until he had both absorbed Eliot and written his now famous poem "A Pact," which is indeed a kind pact with Whitman. (It was very like Pound to form a pact—a two-sided argument—with a famous poet who was dead.) In the poem, he was much more accepting of his filial debt to Whitman than Eliot had been (though Eliot did finally manage to say some good things about Whitman).

> *I make a pact with you, Walt Whitman—*
> *I have detested you long enough.*
> *I come to you as a grown child*
> *Who has had a pig-headed father;*
> *I am old enough now to make friends.*
> *It was you that broke the new wood,*
> *Now is a time for carving.*
> *We have one sap and one root—*
> *Let there be commerce between us.*

That "commerce" found its fruition in the *Cantos* in the same kind of dissociative structure as Eliot's and Whitman's. Pound's pact was in truth between both Whitman and Eliot, who had demonstrated how Whitman's discoveries could be embodied in "modern" poems.

Others

▨ Whitman's influence on contemporary American poetry has been fundamental: his vision is evidenced most vividly in poets like Galway Kinnell and Allen Ginsberg, who both have acknowledged Whitman's inspiring example. But in truth much the greater portion of significant poetry that's been written in America in the last century manifests some aspect of Whitman's music and of his conceptual dimensions. Much of this has been acknowledged: two entire anthologies of American poems have been published honoring Whitman, and celebrating the liberating power of his work.*

And his impact hasn't been limited to American poetry—his influence has been huge, and hugely

---

* *Walt Whitman: The Measure of His Song*, edited by Jim Perlman, Ed Folsom and Dan Campion (Duluth, MN: Holy Cow Press, 1998); and *Visiting Walt*, edited by Sheila Coghill and Thom Tammaro (Iowa City: University of Iowa Press, 2003).

salutary, on poets all over the world. It may well be, in fact, that his influence has been more profound in the rest of the world even than in his own country. Pablo Neruda, the most celebrated Spanish language poet of the twentieth century, wrote an "Ode to Walt Whitman" in which he says:

> *And Walt did not disdain*
> *all the gifts of the earth,*
> *the capital's surfeit of curves,*
> *the purple initial of learning,*
> *but taught me to be an americano,*
> *& raised my eyes to books,*
> *toward the treasure that we find*
> *inside a kernel of wheat*
>
> (Translated by Greg Simon)

And the great Portuguese, Fernando Pessoa, who divided himself into four distinct poetic identities, each with his own name and character, wrote in the most exuberant of them a long panegyric, "Salutation to Walt Whitman," in which he cries:

> *He's called Walt:*
>
> *Entryway to everything!*
> *Bridge to everything!*
> *Highway to everything!*
> *Your omnivorous soul,*

Your soul that's bird, fish, beast, man, woman,
Your soul that's two where two exist,
Your soul that's one becoming two when two
  are one,
Your soul that's arrow, lightning, space,
Amplex, nexus, sex and Texas, Carolina and
  New York,
Brooklyn Ferry in the twilight,
Brooklyn Ferry going back and forth,
Libertad! Democracy! The Twentieth Century
  about to dawn!
Boom! Boom! Boom! Boom!
BOOM!

(Translated Edwin Honig
and Susan M. Brown)

Might it be that Pessoa's infatuation with
Whitman had something to do with his deciding
to disintegrate himself into different poets as he
did? A good part of Whitman's greatness resides
in his fusions, his amalgamations of clearly dis-
parate spiritual dimensions. Could being aware
of Whitman's hugeness have intimidated Pessoa,
made him realize there was no way to arrive at
equivalent dimensions, and that perhaps if he
took himself apart, and assembled the identities
he could find in himself, he might at least make a

facsimile of one poet out of the sum of the others who'd equal Whitman's diversity of inspiration?

The Syrian-Lebanese poet Adonis, who brought Arabic poetry into the twentieth century, acknowledged his debt to Whitman. In "The Funeral of New York" he writes:

> Walt Whitman,
> I see letters careening toward you
> down the streets of Manhattan . . .
> And you, Walt Whitman,
> stay exiled like an immigrant.
> Have you become a bird unknown in the
>   American sky?
> Whitman,
> let our turn be now.
> Let's make a ladder with our visions,
> weave a common pillow with our footsteps . . .
>   (Translated by Samuel Hazo)

The Turkish communist poet Nazim Hikmet, the Russian Vladimir Mayakovsky . . . This is only to mention a few: the list is vast of those whose very poetic identities would have been impossible without Whitman.

Neruda, in a speech to PEN in New York in 1972, stated what might serve as an *ars poetica* for all of those who found inspiration in Whitman:

I must start by acknowledging myself to be the humble servant of a poet who strode the earth with long, slow paces. . . . This great man, this lyric moralist, chose a hard path for himself: he was both a terrestrial and a didactic singer—qualities which appear opposed. . . . He was the first totalitarian poet: his intention was not just to sing, but to impose on others his own total and wide-ranging vision of the relationships of men and nations. . . .Walt Whitman has taught me more than Spain's Cervantes: in Walt Whitman's work one never finds the ignorant being humbled, nor is the human condition ever found offended.

The Body

Almost the first thing that strikes me each time I read Whitman is how unique his poem's relation is to his body, his flesh, his senses. In the poems he *possesses* his body, rather than merely inhabiting it, in a way no one else does, in literature, and as far as I can tell, in life. He uses his body, and he allows his body to use him, or perhaps compels his body to use him, but the relation between self and body is never oppressive, and never abashed. He plunges through his senses like a rapt creature of the deep, he lets his senses lift him, soar him, sail him through the tactile sensuality implicit in every body, but which other bodies all seem too busy, too preoccupied, to pay that much attention to. His body inhales the world, ingests it; he devours reality with eyes and ears and nose and tongue, and always in a way in which all that passes through him is elevated, enhanced, intensified. Who has so registered the pure rapture of sense unmeditated, untransfigured? *"If I worship any particular thing it shall be some of the spread of my body,"* he proclaims, and means it. And goes on in a remarkable passage of diffusion and personification:

> *Translucent mould of me it shall be you,*
> *Shaded ledges and rests, firm masculine*
> *   coulter, it shall be you,*
> *Whatever goes to the tilth of me it shall be*
> *   you,*
> *You my rich blood, your milky stream pale*
> *   strippings of my life;*
> *Breast that presses against other breasts it*
> *   shall be you,*
> *My brain it shall be your occult convolutions,*
> *Root of washed sweet-flag, timorous pond-*

> snipe, nest of guarded duplicate eggs, it
>   shall be you,
> Mixed tussled hay of head and beard and
>   brawn it shall be you,
> Tricking sap of maple, fibre of manly wheat, it
>   shall be you;
> Sun so generous it shall be you,
> Vapors lighting and shading my face it shall
>   be you,
> You sweaty brooks and dews it shall be you,
> Winds whose soft-tickling genitals rub against
>   me it shall be you,
> Broad muscular fields, branches of liveoak,
>   loving lounger in my winding paths, it
>   shall be you,
> Hands I have taken, face I have kissed, mortal
>   I have never touched it shall be you.

And climaxes it all with,

> I dote on myself . . . . there is that lot of me,
>   and all so luscious,
> Each moment and whatever happens thrills
>   me with joy.

And that marvelous title, which came later, "I
Sing the Body Electric," and a whole poem that
is like a series of musical variations on the flesh

of men and women, its evolution, its enactments in human adventures, its sheer factuality—*"in the head the allbaffling brain"*—and the flesh in the world.

As for the body of the world, of existence—Whitman isn't trying to raise reality through his poetry to another level of being, another realm of possibility: his poetry embodies rather the gigantic illuminations that are evident in perception. Unlike Rilke's earth that desires only to be transformed; unlike Traherne's "The corn was orient and immortal wheat," Whitman's vegetation is itself, his poems don't need or want a mode of existence that depends on transformation: his metaphoric stuff is inherent to his perceptions; rather than using mind to alter reality, he finds ways to enlarge the underused senses of the mind, to fling the eyes and ears open wider, to make more sensitive the endings of the nerves.

Those often oddly vague sexual encounters in which the partner is always indeterminate; that brilliantly metaphored sequence of masturbation, in which the figments of guilt and shame, at least in the earlier versions of the poems, are simply driven past by the burgeoning ecstasies of sexual self-acceptance; in all of it the delight is frank, bold, direct.

It doesn't take Whitman long in his poem to assert that the body is going to be a key theme. In the fourth section, after his rapture about the perfumes in houses, he moves to the air which encloses us.

> *The atmosphere is not a perfume . . . . it has no*
> *   taste of the distillation . . . . it is odorless,*
> *It is for my mouth forever . . . . I am in love*
> *   with it,*
> *I will go to the bank by the wood and become*
> *   undisguised and naked,*
> *I am mad for it to be in contact with me.*

Sense, sensation, rapture:

> *The smoke of my own breath,*
> *Echoes, ripples, and buzzed whispers . . . .*
> *   loveroot, silkthread, crotch and vine,*
> *My respiration and inspiration . . . . the*
> *   beating of my heart . . . . the passing of*
> *   blood and air through my lungs . . .*

And then, another persistent theme through the poem, the body shared with other bodies, with not even a transition to get there.

> *The sound of the belched words of my voice . . . .*
> *   words loosed to the eddies of the wind,*

> *A few light kisses . . . . a few embraces . . . .*
> *a reaching around of arms . . .*

Another body, *the* other body, even if nameless, is always there in the poem, to be referred to, exalted, embraced, enjoyed, loved.

He possesses the bodies of others just as he possesses his own. He announces, in "Starting from Paumanok,"

> *Behold, the body includes and is the meaning,*
> *the main concern, and includes and is the*
> *soul;*
> *Whoever you are, how superb and how divine*
> *is your body, or any part of it!*
>
> *(LG, 1860)*

There are countless examples of his beholding with enormous, voluptuous, though not, in every case, sexual delight in the flesh of others; and enormous sympathy, too, for the stricken bodies of others in their suffering or dismay. In "I Sing the Body Electric," is a particularly remarkable example of this:

> *Do you know so much that you call the slave*
> *or the dullface ignorant . . . .*
> *Do you think matter has cohered together*
> *from its diffused float, and*

the soil is on the surface and water runs and
 vegetation sprouts for you . . . . and not for
 him and her?

A slave at auction!
I help the auctioneer . . . . the sloven does not
 half know his business.

Gentlemen look on this curious creature,
Whatever the bids of the bidders they cannot
 be high enough for him,
For him the globe lay preparing quintillions of
 years without one animal or plant,
For him the revolving cycles truly and steadily
 rolled.

In the head the allbaffling brain,
In it and below it the making of the attributes
 of heroes.

         (*LG*, 1855, 1867)

There follows a metaphorical dissection of the slave's body to make manifest the wonders of physical existence.

And another anecdote in "Song of Myself" is a different sort of study of the body. It concerns a woman, alone, surely, a "spinster" probably, watching from her window the "*twenty-eight young* men" who "*bathe by the shore.*" "*Twenty-eight years of womanly life and all so lonesome.*"

It's worth quoting the whole passage, one of the most poignant in all the poems, to see how Whitman evokes the bodies of the men, the longing sensuality of the woman, and the coming together of her fantasy with the vivid reality of their matter.

> *Which of the young men does she like the*
> *   best?*
> *Ah the homeliest of them is beautiful to her.*
>
> *Where are you off to, lady? for I see you,*
> *You splash in the water there, yet stay stock*
> *   still in your room.*
>
> *Dancing and laughing along the beach came*
> *   the twenty-ninth bather,*
> *The rest did not see her, but she saw them and*
> *   loved them.*
>
> *The beards of the young men glistened with*
> *   wet, it ran from their long hair,*
> *Little streams passed all over their bodies.*
>
> *An unseen hand also passed over their bodies,*
> *It descended tremblingly from their temples*
> *   and ribs.*

> *The young men float on their back, their white*
>   *bellies swell to the sun . . . .*

And then one of those lines whose meaning is subject to various interpretations—it could be a reference to the woman's sexual fantasies; or it could be her sagging into her own sadness at the futility of such fleshless imaginings—but which has a force all the more potent for its uncertainty.

> *They do not ask who seizes fast to them,*
> *They do not know who puffs and declines with*
>   *pendant and bending arch,*
> *They do not think whom they souse with spray.*

And the most self-fulfilled bodies, too, Whitman adores. Only a few lines after those of the woman caught in her fantasy, a few pages past the miserable escaping slave, comes an image of masculine confidence, competence, power; another black man, this one a forceful, elemental presence.

> *The negro holds firmly the reins of his four*
>   *horses . . . .*
> *The negro that drives the huge dray of the*
>   *stone yard . . . . steady and tall he stands*
>   *poised on one leg on the stringpiece,*

His blue shirt exposes his ample neck and
*   breast and loosens over his hipband,*
His glance is calm and commanding . . . . he
*   tosses the slouch of his hat away from his*
*   forehead,*
The sun falls on his crispy hair and
*   moustache . . . . falls on the black of his*
*   polished and perfect limbs.*

I behold the picturesque giant and love
*   him . . . .*

This passage, too, has one of those bizarre, wonderfully uninterpretable phrases, as its ending.

In me the caresser of life wherever moving . . . .
*   backward as well as forward sluicing,*
To niches aside and junior bending.

And, near the end of the "Song of Myself," after all the recitations and incantations concerning the flesh of self and the flesh of others, the body of the poet becomes transfigured into something both corporeal and beyond it, his body becomes something like spirit, but, in never renouncing its materiality, something even more.

I depart as air . . . . I shake my white locks at
*   the runaway sun,*

*I effuse my flesh in eddies and drift it in lacy
jags.*

Sex

*As a boy and young man I myself went into
respectable middle-class homes and found
there volumes of Whitman's* Leaves of Grass
*with the so-called ugly and lustful passages
cut out with scissors.*
—Sherwood Anderson

The "good parts" we used to call them in those
antique days of the 1950s when adolescents would
comb through books for any hint that there was
really such a thing as sex outside of one's fever-
ish fantasies, and that there might be a language
to depict it—even, god forbid, celebrate it. All of
society seemed to object to anything remotely
like that. Remember when Norman Mailer's *The
Naked and the Dead* was published, and the word
"fuck," the central word of any real soldier's vo-
cabulary, had to be euphemized as "fug"? *Everything* sexual and sensual was encoded then, everything of real interest.

Boys then didn't know about Whitman—maybe he was kept from us. Would he have been in our junior high school library, during those years we were all but imploding with sexual obsession and ignorance? I doubt it. *The Portable Walt Whitman* was the first book of poetry I ever bought for myself, when I was sixteen. I've often wondered what it was that drew me to it: might I have opened it in the book section of our town's department store, and come upon those dumbfounding lines?

> *I do not press my finger across my mouth,*
> *I keep as delicate around the bowels as*
> *   around the head and heart,*
> *Copulation is no more rank to me than*
> *   death is.*

The sexuality in *Leaves of Grass* tends to be considered in terms of how revolutionary it was for Whitman's time, how he broke down and through the violent repressions of the Victorian era, and of course he well knew that's what he was up to. In the lines that precede those, he forthrightly proclaims it:

> *Through me forbidden voices,*
> *Voices of seizes and lusts . . . . voices veiled,*
> *   and I remove the veil.*

> *Voices indecent by me clarified and*
> *transfigured.*

Not long before he died he even went so far as to say about the *Leaves* to Traubel: "Sex is the root of it all. Sex—the coming together of men and women: sex: sex."

All well and good, and he did, really, finally, do it for us: who else, even from the perspective of the sexually "liberated" culture of America in the sixties and seventies, did it better? I was there for the sexual revolution, I saw the young people tear off their clothes and dance; I even wanted to do it myself, but I was shy. How not think of Whitman with all that? Who else were the revolution's real ancestors but Whitman and his heirs, the beats, the hippies, the commune-dwellers, and the organizers of festivals, which tried to enact at least a semblance of a Whitmanian ecstatic communality, acceptance, communion, merge. If there were other antecedents, no one said it so well, no one came so close to sanctioning it as rapturously as did Whitman. Sadly it didn't, couldn't, fundamentally change our anxieties, our propensity for aggression, our basic instinctual conflicts. But it did definitely realign the mores of Western culture, most profoundly I suppose American culture, which had inherited a more repressed puritanical tradition than most countries in the West. When I think back to that time now, it's impossible not to imagine Whitman quietly presiding.

Still, most remarkable to me when I read the poems again isn't their social-revolutionary implications, but rather their exultant sensual exuberance, the unabashed (to say the least) delight Whitman is able to convey about sex, how large the pleasure his character takes in the sexual, and how the erotic is extended out past body, past psyche, to eroticize all of reality. It's that which remains most radical for me—how well he depicts the ecstasy beyond mere act, mere thought of act.

And of course there's the way he poeticizes it. Sometimes the sensual seems to be driven directly out of the sounds of his language, of the vowel and consonant themselves, as though so much voluptuousness of sound of necessity must entail the erotic. This passage, ostensibly about sunrise, begins with some of those lines the precise meaning of which can only be guessed at:

> *Hefts of the moving world at innocent*
> *gambols, silently rising, freshly exuding,*
> *Scooting obliquely high and low.*

> *Something I cannot see puts upward libidi-*
> *   nous prongs,*
> *Seas of bright juice suffuse heaven.*

"Libidinous prongs!" "Bright juice!" The poem, the poet, overflows with the subtle and not subtle sensualities of perception itself.

There's another passage that's a love-sex poem to earth and to ocean. One line is particularly gorgeously sensual, too: "Earth of the vitreous pour of the full moon just tinged with blue!" The engagement with the earth then becomes frankly sexualized:

> *Far-swooping elbowed earth! Rich apple-*
> *   blossomed earth!*
> *Smile, for your lover comes!*
>
> *Prodigal! you have given me love! . . . .*
> *   therefore I to you give love!*
> *O unspeakable passionate love!*
>
> *Thruster holding me tight and that I hold*
> *   tight!*
> *We hurt each other as the bridegroom and the*
> *   bride hurt each other!*

Preposterous that figuration, yet in context reasonable, and just. And then the sea is addressed, as though it might be jealous of that other consummation:

> You sea! I resign myself to you also I
>   guess what you mean,
> I behold from the beach your crooked inviting
>   fingers,
> I believe you refuse to go back without feeling
>   of me,
> We must have a turn together . . . . I undress . . . .
>   hurry me out of sight of the land,
> Cushion me soft . . . . rock me in billow drowse,
> Dash me with amorous wet . . . . I can repay
>   you!

In "Spontaneous Me," from 1856, another paean to sexuality, he all but outrageously eroticizes a sipping bee.

> The hairy wild-bee that murmurs and
>   hankers up and down, that grips the
>   full-grown lady-flower, curves upon her
>   with amorous firm legs, takes his will of
>   her, and holds himself tremulous and tight
>   until he is satisfied

Has creature-world ever been so alluringly transported to the realm of Eros?

Sometimes the poems' sexual procedures move in very different directions. An anecdote from 1855, in the section ultimately entitled "The Sleepers," revolves around the poet's imaginary union with a woman, who is receiving an illegitimate lover; the woman in turn emotionally doubles herself, then her lover to some other entity, named "darkness," who might be the poet, the lover, the actual dark, the fantasy of the fantasized woman: great confusion, not really able to be definitively clarified, but, again, all of the reality that contains these tumultuous goings-on still will end up generating a delectable sensualization of the primary emotions of attending, waiting, anticipating.

> *I am she who adorned herself and folded her*
>   *hair expectantly,*
> *My truant lover has come and it is dark.*
>
> *Double yourself and receive me darkness,*
> *Receive me and my lover too . . . . he will not*
>   *let me go without him.*
>
> *I roll myself upon you as upon a bed . . . . I*
>   *resign myself to the dusk.*
>
> *He whom I call answers me and takes the*
>   *place of my lover,*
> *He rises with me silently from the bed.*

Darkness you are gentler than my lover . . . .
    his flesh was sweaty and panting,
I feel the hot moisture yet that he left me . . . .

Be careful, darkness . . . . already, what was it
    touched me?
I thought my lover had gone . . . . else darkness
    and he are one,
I hear the heart-beat . . . . I follow . . I fade
    away.

But, at the end—almost too grievous to believe—
we're plunged into a tragedy, what sounds like a
terribly real one, with an awful outcome: expo-
sure, shame, distress, and despair.

O hotcheecked and blushing! O foolish hectic!
O for pity's sake, no one must see me
    now! . . . . my clothes were stolen while I
    was abed,
Now I am thrust forth, where shall I run?

So, even a woman's shame. And even the shame
around masturbation, which as I mentioned before, is both used as a figure of acute pleasure and
literally recounted. The delight in listening to a soprano singing is so heightened that it's equated with
the helpless, guilty intensity of self-pleasuring.

I hear the trained soprano . . . . she convulses
  me like the climax of my love-grip.

You villain touch! what are you doing? . . . .
  my breath is tight in its throat;
Unclench your floodgates! you are too much
  for me.

Blind loving wrestling touch! Sheathed hooded
  sharptoothed touch!
Did it make you ache so leaving me?

And, in another poem, masturbation is evoked in itself; the act that comes upon the young and takes them, despite their futile reluctance.

The young man that flushes and flushes, and
  the young woman that flushes and flushes,
The young man that wakes deep at night, the
  hot hand seeking to repress what would
  master him,
The mystic amorous night, the strange
  half-welcome pants, visions, sweats,
The pulse pounding through palms and
  trembling encircling fingers, the young man
  all color'd red, ashamed, angry . . .
    (*LG*, "Spontaneous Me," 1867)

Gerard Manley Hopkins occurs to me here. In a famous letter to his friend Robert Bridges, Hopkins said of Whitman: "I always knew in my heart Walt Whitman's mind to be more like my own than any other man's living. As he is a great scoundrel this is not a pleasant confession." His distaste is generally read as having its impetus in Hopkins's suspected homosexuality, which he very successfully repressed, but I wonder if he might have been even more shocked and dismayed by Whitman's frankness about masturbation, which would have been a particularly delicate subject for a lifelong celibate? I certainly don't know of anyone else who had written before Whitman (and not much after) about masturbation so frankly and graphically.*

Whitman didn't limit his sexuality to the private, the furtive, the sublimated. He wanted everything, every aspect of it, every pleasure he could find in it. In the eighth part of the "clus-

* The rest of Hopkins's letter to Bridges consists of one of the many explications of his own metrical innovations, comparing them this time to Whitman's. Sounding challenged by the only real competitor in sight, he tries to demonstrate that although Whitman's music is "interesting," he is really only writing "rhythmic prose." He goes on, as though coming to himself, "The above remarks are not meant to run down Whitman."

ter," as he called them, of the poems of "Enfans d'Adam," he shouts:

> *Give me now libidinous joys only!*
> *Give me the drench of my passions! Give me*
> *   life coarse and rank!*
> *To-day, I go consort with nature's darlings—*
> *   to-night too,*
> *I am for those who believe in loose delights—I*
> *   share the midnight orgies of young men,*
> *I dance with the dancers, and drink with the*
> *   drinkers,*
> *The echoes ring with our indecent calls,*
> *I take for my love some prostitute—I pick out*
> *   some low person for my dearest friend . . .*
>
> (LG, 1860)

And a few poems later in the same series proclaims:

> *Ages and ages, returning at intervals,*
> *Undestroyed, wandering immoral,*
> *Lusty, phallic, with the potent original loins,*
> *   perfectly sweet,*
> *I, chanter of Adamic songs,*
> *Through the new garden, the West, the great*
> *   cities, calling,*
> *Deliriate, thus prelude what is generated,*
> *   offering these, offering myself,*

Bathing myself, bathing my songs in sex,
Offspring of my loins.

And from the 1856 edition, in "Poem of Procreation," later called "A Woman Waits for Me," he
goes almost deliriously mad with it all.

Sex contains all, bodies, souls,
Meanings, proofs, purities, delicacies, results,
*   promulgations,*
Songs, commands, health, pride, the maternal
*   mystery, the seminal milk,*
All hopes, benefactions, bestowals, all the
*   passions, loves, beauties, delights of the*
*   earth,*
All the governments, judges, gods, follow'd
*   persons of the earth,*
These are contained in sex as parts of itself
*   and justifications of self.*

Hurray!

Woman

He worships women, almost literally; he de-
lightedly, all but obsessively accumulates evidence
of their tenderness, their beauty, their strength,

their existential equality with men, beginning with his mother, his "perfect mother," as he calls her.[*] Whitman was deeply aware of women's questions, recognizing women's exploitation, their victimhood, the fact that wages for women were so low that for some prostitution was the only recourse. But it has to be said that at the same time as Whitman was calling for women's equality with men, he was ambivalent about "women's rights," and in his support for women's right to vote, proclaimed with less than perfect enthusiasm: "The day is coming when the deep questions of woman's entrance amid the arenas of practical life politics, the suffrage, &c., will not only be argued . . . but may be put to decision, and real experiment."

And in the poems, though he seems to glorify womanly identity, it is usually, if not always, in terms of women's maternal capacities, of their task of birthing and nurturing great, greater Americans; a "sane athletic maternity," he calls it. This was a common attitude at the time, when

---

[*] At first it's a bit disquieting to come upon the tintype of the actual Louisa, supremely homely, fiercely coiffed, but regarded again not fiercely visaged; a bit of wryness around what looks like a toothless mouth, a wisdom-squint around the eyes. Father beside her, compared to her, looks disappointed, dour.

there was a movement called "Real Womanhood."
The most fervent, and somewhat odd, expression
of this attitude in Whitman is in the (very weak)
poem "Unfolded Out of the Folds."

> *Unfolded out of the folds of the woman man*
>   *comes unfolded, and is always to come*
>   *unfolded,*
> *Unfolded only out of the superbest woman of*
>   *the earth is to come the superbest man of*
>   *the earth . . . .*
> *Unfolded out of the perfect body of a woman*
>   *can a man be form'd of perfect body,*
> *Unfolded only out of the inimitable poems of*
>   *woman can come the poems of man, (only*
>   *thence have my poems come;)*
> *Unfolded out of the strong and arrogant*
>   *woman I love, only thence can appear the*
>   *strong and arrogant man I love,*
> *Unfolded by brawny embraces from the*
>   *well-muscled woman I love, only thence*
>   *come the brawny embraces of the man.*
> *Unfolded out of the justice of the woman all*
>   *justice is unfolded . . . .*
> *First the man is shaped in the woman, he can*
>   *then be shaped in himself.*

> (*LG*, 1856)

Yet women, in general and as characters in anecdotes, are everywhere in his work, and there are also clear expressions of what would come to be termed a modern view of athletic femininity. In "Poem of Procreation," from 1856, in later editions entitled "A Woman Waits for Me," he writes:

> They are not one jot less than I am,
> They are tanned in the face by shining suns
> and blowing winds,
> Their flesh has the old divine suppleness and
> strength,
> They know how to swim, row, ride, wrestle,
> shoot, run, strike, retreat, advance, resist,
> defend themselves,
> They are ultimate in their own right—they are
> calm, clear, well-possessed of themselves.

The recognition and acknowledgment of the unqualified presence of women, in a noncondescending, nonromantic way, is key to Whitman's larger vision. Woman is *present,* he insists time and again, not as novelistic victim, not as *Belle Dame Sans Merci,* but as herself. Whitman's women have a forcefulness, a resoluteness: woman is here in power, and suffering, in assertion and betrayal.

> *I am the poet of the woman the same as the*
> *man,*
> *And I say it is as great to be a woman as to be*
> *a man.*
>
> (LG, 1856)

And from what come later to be entitled "The Song for Occupations":

> *The wife—and she is not one jot less than the*
> *husband,*
> *The daughter—and she is just as good as the*
> *son,*
> *The mother—and she is every bit as much as*
> *the father.*

And in "To Think of Time" appears woman in her purely sexual identity:

> *the pleasure of men with women shall never*
> *be sated . . nor the pleasure of women with*
> *men . . .*

To speak frankly of "the pleasure of women with men" in the century of Queen Victoria was something not often done, in poetry or anywhere else. Yet it is the case that many of the ideas that encouraged Whitman to give women such a key role in the poems were current in the thought and literature of even the high popular culture of his time—for decades there had been women political lecturers and orators, propagandists for suffrage, equality, even free love. Whitman heard many of them speak and knew some personally, and his poems impart an aura of essential energy and propulsion to women that contradicted their passive image in most nineteenth-century literature and art, and for the most part in society.

The effect of Whitman on women poets in the United States has been profound, not so much because of his promulgations of women's rights, or his hymns to them in the poems, but because of his poetry itself. Alicia Ostriker, in a brilliant essay, "Loving Walt Whitman and the Problem of America," offers what I think is the most cogent view of how an intelligent, formidable poet regards Whitman. "What moves me," Ostriker writes,

> and I suspect other American women poets, is less the agreeable programmatic utterances than the gestures whereby Whitman enacts the crossing of gender categories in his own person. It is not his claim to be "of the woman" that speeds us on our way, but his capacity to be shamelessly re-

ceptive as well as active, to be expansive on an epic scale without a shred of nostalgia for narratives of conquest, to invent a rhetoric of power without authority, without hierarchy, and without violence. The omnivorous empathy of his imagination wants to incorporate All, and therefore refuses to represent anything as unavailably Other. So long as femaleness in our culture signifies Otherness, Walt's greed is our gain. In him we are freed to be what we actually are, in whatever portion of ourselves eludes society, system and philosophy: not negative pole to positive pole, not adversarial half of some dichotomy, but figures in an energetic dance.

It can't be stated more cogently than that. Ostriker's poems, and the work of many contemporary woman poets, manifest, sometimes subtly, sometimes overtly, the influence of Whitman, the power of his grand vision for all poetry, all poets.

Lorca, Ginsberg, and "The Faggots"

◉ Here is Lorca, from his "Ode to Walt Whitman," in *Poeta en Nueva York*:

> *He's one, too! That's right! And they land*
> *on your luminous chaste beard,*
> *blonds from the north, blacks from the*
>   *sands . . .*
> *the faggots, Walt Whitman, the faggots . . .*
>   (translated by Greg Simon
>   and Steven F. White)

Lorca's entire poem is an homage to the variousness of Whitman's subject matter, to his broad field of vision, but he most fervently admires Whitman for his expressions of homosexual love; Whitman rescues him, he implies, and homosexuality itself from the dark, derogatory world whose very languages are contaminated by loathing. The poem goes on to enumerate pejoratives in other countries:

> *Always against you, who give boys*
> *drops of foul death with bitter poison.*
> *Always against you,*
> Fairies *of North America,*
> Pájaros *of Havana,*

Jotos *of Mexico,*
Sarasas *of Cadiz,*
Aprios *of Sevilla…*

And, only a generation or so later, here's Allen Ginsberg, in "A Supermarket in California":

I saw you, Walt Whitman, childless, lonely old
grubber, poking among the meats in the
refrigerator and eyeing the grocery boys . . .

Ah, dear father, graybeard, lonely old
courage-teacher . . .

"Courage-teacher" is what Whitman surely was for Ginsberg, and has remained so for the homosexual community. As Mark Doty puts it in his essay, "Form, Eros, and the Unspeakable": "What is not at all vague are the needs which Whitman's poems met, the powerful voice they gave or loaned to an emergent class of men who had felt themselves isolated and voiceless."

Love among men occurs again and again in the poems, sometimes as expressions of comradely affection, sometimes seeming to state frankly and passionately homosexual experiences. The cluster of poems titled "Calamus" is to a great extent a paean to all forms of love, but particularly among males.

Here to put your lips upon mine I permit you;
With the comrade's long-dwelling kiss, or the
new husband's kiss,
For I am the new husband, and I am the
comrade . . . "

O here I last saw him that tenderly loves
me—and returns again, never to separate
from me . . .

For the one I love most lay sleeping by me
under the same cover in the cool night,
In the stillness, in the autumn moonbeams,
his face was inclined toward me,
And his arm lay lightly around my breast—
And that night I was happy.

Yet, despite what would seem to be the clearest evidence in just these few lines among many others, during his lifetime there was disagreement among some of Whitman's admirers about whether Whitman was actually what we now would call "homosexual" (a word that didn't then exist). Some vehemently rejected the very thought; some, especially those who were themselves engaged in same-sex relationships, welcomed his sanctioning of what Whitman called, a bit ambiguously, "a new friendship."

Whitman himself seemed later in life to enjoy dancing around the subject, most notably in his much cited reply to a letter of John Addington Symonds, who, though he had fathered four children, was an avid homosexual; who had been after Whitman indirectly for years about the apparent homosexuality in the "Calamus" poems, and finally confronted him head on. Whitman objected, saying that Symonds's "morbid inferences" about the poems were "damnable" and "disavowed by me," and to prove his heterosexuality he claimed to have fathered six children by various women. There's no evidence of this whatsoever, and his being able to claim it might be put down to the trivial dementia of fame, the realizing that the self who seemed to be being publicly admired, all but worshipped, had essentially nothing to do with who he himself really was, and that the past can be contingent, malleable, to be generated or deleted as occasion or mood demands. On the other hand, he may simply have been teasing Symonds about his own complicated sexual history.

But that Whitman had passionate relationships with men is without doubt—there are references in the poems and prose to encounters with young men, as in the section of "Crossing Brooklyn Ferry," in which Whitman iterates his doubts and self-hatred, but tempers them with the positive experiences of male contact.

> *Was call'd by my nighest name by clear loud*
> *voices of young men as they saw me*
> *approaching or passing,*
> *Felt their arms on my neck as I stood, or the*
> *negligent leaning of their flesh against me*
> *as I sat,*
> *Saw many I loved in the street or ferry-boat*
> *or public assembly, yet never told them a*
> *word . . .*

And even if Whitman preferred later in his life to remain ambiguous about whether he ever actually experienced homosexual sex, there are passages in the manuscripts that are much more definite. In an early manuscript version of sections twenty-eight and twenty-nine of "Song of Myself" for instance, Whitman writes:

> *Grip'd Wrestler! Do you keep your heaviest*
> *grip for the last?*
> *Must you bite with your teeth with the worst*
> *spasms at parting? . . . .*

> *Little as your mouth is, it has drained me dry*
> *of my strength.*[*]

Beyond this, the relations between males that Whitman depicts in the poems portray a depth of emotion between men that is as affecting as anything ever written on the theme. In one of the "Calamus" poems, in another passage about doubt, of everything, "the terrible question of appearances," the dread and anxieties of the speaker are finally resolved in a moving description of the emotions of lovers, of how such emotions of affection can temper the anguish of depressive feelings:

> *To me, these, [his doubts] and the like of*
> *these, are curiously answered by my lovers,*
> *my dear friends;*
> *When he whom I love travels with me, or sits*
> *a long while holding me by the hand,*
> *When the subtle air, the impalpable, the sense*
> *that words and reason hold not, surround*
> *and pervade us,*
>
> *Then I am charged with untold and untellable*
> *wisdom—I am silent—I require nothing*
> *further,*

* Quoted in Robert Martin, *The Homosexual Tradition in American Poetry* (Iowa City: University of Iowa Press, 1998), p. 28.

I cannot answer the question of appearances,
*   or that of identity beyond the grave,*
But I walk or sit indifferent—I am satisfied,
He ahold of my hand has completely satisfied
*   me.*

                    ("Calamus" cluster, 1860)

And, in another "Calamus" poem, he writes:

And when I thought how my dear friend, my
*   lover, was on his way coming, O then I was*
*   happy . . .*

And in still another, there is certainly evidence of passionate affection, at the very least.

Consuming, burning for his love whom I love!

Whitman's claim to have had heterosexual experiences has never been completely resolved. There's a letter from 1962 to Whitman pseudonymously signed "Ellen Eyre" that some take to be evidence of a sexual experience, particularly the sentence, "I trust you will think well enough of me to renew the pleasure you afforded me last p.m.," but I find this hardly compelling. It might well be the compliment of a not well-educated woman flattered by the attention of such a powerful emotional and intellectual personality.

There are also several passages in which Whitman recounts making love with women, but it's difficult to tell whether they're just more of his abundant fictions. In "From Pent Up Aching Rivers," which Whitman had considered calling "Song of Procreation," if what he reports is fictional, he certainly wants the passage to sound like the testimony of someone who has experienced procreative sex.

> *It is I, you women—I make my way,*
> *I am stern, acrid, large, undissuadable—but I*
> *love you,*
> *I do not hurt you any more than is necessary*
> *for you,*
> *I pour the stuff to start my sons and daughters*
> *fit for These States—I press with slow rude*
> *muscle,*
> *I brace myself effectually—I listen to no*
> *entreaties,*
> *I dare not withdraw till I deposit what has so*
> *long accumulated within me.*
>
> (*LG*, 1860)

Finally, though, the words have a rather programmatic, not very authentic sounding vehemence.

It was once thought that Whitman had an affair with a woman during his time in New Orleans, because of a passage in "Once I Pass'd through a Populous City" that at first sight speaks quite clearly of something like that.

> *Yet now, of all that city I remember only a*
>   *woman I casually met there, who detained*
>   *me for love of me,*
> *Day by day and night by night we were*
>   *together,—All else has long been forgotten*
>   *by me,*
> *I remember I say only that woman who*
>   *passionately clung to me,*
> *Again we wander—we love—we separate*
>   *again,*
> *Again she holds me by the hand—I must not*
>   *go!*
> *I see her close beside me, with silent lips, sad*
>   *and tremulous.*
>
>   *(LG, 1860)*

However, an earlier draft of the passage reads very differently:

> *But now of all that city I remember only the*
>   *man who wandered with me there, for love*
>   *of me,*
> *Day by day and night by night we were*
>   *together.*

All else has long been forgotten by me—I
remember, I say, only one rude and
ignorant man who, when I departed, long
and long held me by the hand, with silent
lips, sad and tremulous.

Whitman's reticence, or outright deceptive-ness, later in his life on the subject was inconsis-tent, to say the least. It's often been pointed out that male love, not necessarily homosexual love, was accepted during that time in a way not many decades later it wasn't: men embracing, kissing, calling each "lover," was apparently common-place. In fact, when *Leaves of Grass* was "banned in Boston," it was because of the passages of het-erosexual eroticism, not the portions that could be construed as being homosexual. There's no question that Whitman later on did clearly want to temper the frankness that informed so much of the passages of homosexual experience that he'd recorded during those first years of the poems, but the words are there.

And in the end it hardly matters: the effect of Whitman's poetry on the homosexual commu-nity has had no qualifications. Whitman devised a heartening rhetoric of acceptance and defiance for generations of gay men, and gay women. "Always against you . . . , " Lorca wrote about the disapproving world. " . . . Always against you . . . ," but, thanks in good part to Whitman, no longer morally tenable, no longer to be given credence.

Nature

▓ Don't think of the abstracting spiritual yearnings of Shelley's "Skylark"—

Hail to thee, blithe Spirit!
Bird thou never wert,
That from heaven, or near it,
Pourest thy full heart
In profuse strains of unpremeditated art.

Higher still and higher
From the earth thou springest
Like a cloud of fire;
The blue deep thou wingest,
And singing still dost soar, and soaring ever
    singest.

Rather consider the concrete, well-observed, specific details of John Clare's "Cuckoo"—

The cuckoo, like a hawk in flight,
With narrow pointed wings

Whews o'er our heads—soon out of sight
And as she flies she sings . . . .
I've watched it on an old oak tree
Sing half an hour away
Until its quick eye noticed me
And then it whewed away.
Its mouth when open shone as red
As hips upon the brier,
Like stock doves seemed its winged head
But striving to get higher.

It was with the meticulous attentiveness of Clare that Whitman regarded and recorded natural phenomena. If sometimes, like Shelley, he does get carried away with the metaphysical, symbolic possibilities of his nature watching, still always he manages to maintain an intense, concrete observation of the natural world.

When the snows had melted, and Fifth-month
    grass was growing,
Up this seashore, in some briers,
Two guests from Alabama—two together,
And their nest, and four light-green eggs,
    spotted with brown,
And every day the he-bird, to and fro, near at
    hand,

And every day the she-bird, crouched on her
*   nest, silent, with bright eyes,*
And every day I, a curious boy, never too
*   close, never disturbing them,*
Cautiously peering, absorbing, translating.

This from "A Word Out of the Sea," from
1859, which later was splendidly retitled "Out
of the Cradle Endlessly Rocking," but unluckily
revised down a bit. There follows a passage of
something close to a Romantic rhapsody, not really characteristic of Whitman's normally acute
nature writing, enacting, rather, the imaginative
immaturity with which the boy Walter drama-
tizes the little tragedy that so affects him. Then
back to facts:

Till of a sudden,
May-be killed, unknown to her mate,
One forenoon the she-bird crouched not on
*   the nest,*
Nor returned that afternoon, nor the next,
Nor ever appeard again.

And thenceforward, all summer, in the sound
*   of the sea,*
And at night, under the full of the moon, in
*   calmer weather,*

Over the hoarse surging of the sea,
Or flitting from brier to brier by day,
I saw, I heard at intervals, the remaining one,
    the he-bird,
The solitary guest from Alabama.

Whitman knew and studied Shelley's poems. It's unlikely he'd have known Clare's—almost no one did then—but his passion for the natural world, and for the places where the human touches it, was much closer to Clare's down-to-earth, close-to-the-ground vision, and it suffuses all his work, most often with a purity similar to Clare's, but with a wild exaltation that Clare's verse music couldn't permit. The stressy, surging pulses with which Whitman could inform his perceptions were all new, and all his.

Chaff, straw, splinters of wood, weeds, and the
    sea-gluten,
Scum, scales from shining rocks, leaves of
    salt-lettuce left by the tide . . .
                ("As I Ebb'd with the Ocean of Life,"
                                        LG, 1860)

And his wandering syntax, his phrase-determined rhetoric offered him a more inclusive kind of seeing than anything before him.

My tread scares the wood-drake and wood-
duck on my distant and daylong ramble,
They rise together, they slowly circle around . . . .
I believe in those winged purposes,
And acknowledge the red yellow and white
playing within me,
And consider the green and violet and the
tufted crown intentional,
And do not call the tortoise unworthy because
she is not something else,
And the mockingbird in the swamp never
studied the gamut, yet trills pretty well to
me,
And the look of the bay mare shames silliness
out of me.

The wild gander leads his flock through
the cool night . . .

The sharphoofed moose of the north,
the cat on the housesill, the chickadee,
the prairie-dog,
The litter of the grunting sow as they tug
at her teats,
The brood of the turkeyhen, and she with
her halfspread wings,
I see in them and myself the same old law.

("Song of Myself")

"The same old law"—this is the basic truth with which Whitman use nature to inform his vision. It's what's behind his mingling so thoroughly of natural and human events.

> *Where the quail is whistling betwixt the*
>> *woods and the wheatlot,*
> *Where the bat flies in the July eve . . . .*
>> *where the great goldbug drops through the*
>> *dark;*
> *Where the flails keep time on the barn floor,*
> *Where the brook puts out of the roots of the*
>> *old tree and flows to the meadow,*
> *Where cattle stand and shake away flies with*
>> *the tremulous shuddering of their hides,*
> *Where the cheese-cloth hangs in the kitchen,*
>> *and andirons straddle the hearth-slab, and*
>> *cobwebs fall in festoons from the rafters . . .*

And it's also why the natural world and the world of the self, even the physical self, are so regularly brought into a terrifically intimate connection, as in the section I quoted in "The Body." "*If I worship any particular thing it shall be some of the spread of my body,*" which moves directly, with no more connection than a comma, to a symbolization of the genitals, and the body itself, and farther into nonsymbolic materiality.

He can be especially moving in his evocation of animals. In one passage of the "Song," which has become one of the most quoted in all his work, he proclaims:

> I think I could turn and live awhile with
>   the animals . . . . they are so placid and
>   self-contained,
> I stand and look at them sometimes half the
>   day long.
>
> They do not sweat and whine about their
>   condition,
> They do not lie awake in the dark and weep
>   for their sins,
> They do not make me sick discussing their
>   duty to God,
> Not one is dissatisfied . . . . not one is
>   demented with the mania of owning
>   things,
> Not one kneels to another nor to his kind that
>   lived thousands of years ago,
> Not one is respectable or unhappy over the
>   whole earth.

"Thousands of years ago . . . . " As far as I know, no poet before Whitman took into account and poeticized the new notions of evolutionary time that had only recently become current. It becomes a key part of his physics and metaphysics.

Eternity lies in bottomless reservoirs . . . . its
    buckets are rising forever and ever,
They pour and they pour and they exhale
    away.

We have thus far exhausted trillions of winters
    and summers;
There are trillions ahead, and trillions ahead
    of them.

Births have brought us richness and variety,
And other births will bring us richness and
    variety.

I do not call one greater and one smaller,
That which fills its period and place is equal
    to any . . . .

Rise after rise bow the phantoms behind me,
Afar down I see the huge first Nothing, the
    vapor from the nostrils of death,
I know I was even there . . . . I waited unseen
    and always,
And slept while God carried me through the
    lethargic mist,
And took my time . . . . and took no hurt from
    the foetid carbon.

And he goes on, scientifically, poetically, heart-eningly.

> *Before I was born out of my mother genera-*
> *tions guided me,*
> *My embryo has never been torpid . . . .*
> *nothing could overlay it;*
> *For it the nebula cohered to an orb . . . . the*
> *long slow strata piled to rest it on . . . . vast*
> *vegetables gave it sustenance,*
> *Monstrous sauroids transported it in their*
> *mouths and deposited it with care.*

But it's in their sheer observational force, their precision of detail, their broad and blazing attentiveness that Whitman's poems prove him a great nature poet, as great as Clare, certainly as great as or greater than any other American poet. Here is the poet among still more creatures:

> *Scorched ankle-deep by the hot sand . . . .*
> *hauling my boat down the shallow river;*
> *Where the panther walks to and fro on a*
> *limb overhead . . . . where the buck turns*
> *furiously at the hunter,*
> *Where the rattlesnake suns his flabby length*
> *on a rock . . . . where the otter is feeding*
> *on fish,*

> *Where the alligator in his tough pimples sleeps*
> *by the bayou,*
> *Where the black bear is searching for roots or*
> *honey . . . . where the beaver pats the mud*
> *with his paddle-tail . . .*

He's a great listener as well:

> *Where the quail is whistling betwixt the*
> *woods and the wheatlot . . . .*
> *Where the mockingbird sounds his delicious*
> *gurgles, and cackles and screams and*
> *weeps . . .*

And a powerful evoker of landscape:

> *Of the turbid pool that lies in the autumn*
> *forest,*
> *Of the moon that descends the steeps of the*
> *soughing twilight,*
> *Toss, sparkes of day and dusk . . . . toss on the*
> *black stems that decay in the muck,*
> *Toss to the moaning gibberish of the dry*
> *limbs.*

There's enough evidence everywhere in the poems to prove the remark of Whitman's friend, the great naturalist John Burroughs, that Whitman was "not merely an observer of Nature, but is immersed in her," his poems "approximate to a direct utterance of Nature herself."

Prophets

◈ Once, when I was first considering writing this book, was reading Whitman constantly, and was all but overwhelmed by the poems and the poet, I said to a friend that I thought the person speaking in the *Leaves of Grass* was the most spiritually perfect human being who ever lived. My friend, an admirably clear-eyed intellectual, looked taken aback, and I realized what an absurd thing I'd said. Was *anyone* ever the most spiritually perfect person who ever lived? I thought I never would believe so, but at that moment, still submerged in Whitman's voice, and the psyche behind the voice, the cosmos of the voice, I believed it.

And perhaps it shouldn't be all that surprising, because Whitman had an ambition something like that in the plans for his work. In an unpublished introduction to the 1861 edition, he says his purpose is

> to suggest the substance and form of a large, sane, perfect Human Being or character for

an American man and for woman. While other things are in the book, studies, digressions of various sorts, this is undoubtedly its essential purpose and its key, so that in the poems taken as a whole unquestionably appears a great Person, entirely modern, at least as great as anything in the Homeric or Shakespearian characters, a person with the free courage of Achilles, the craft of Ulysses, the attributes of the Greek deities. Majesty, passion, temper, amativeness, Romeo, Lear, Antony, immense self-esteem, but after democratic forms, measureless love, the old eternal elements of first-class humanity.

Although one has to know all along that the person of the poems is a creation, an impossible project, it's almost sad to read the biographies of the man, and discover that Whitman was a human being, if not like any other, then sharing many of our foibles, self-over-estimations—all of it. But there's one thing at least: there seems to come a time in many literary biographies when the biographer begins to appear disappointed, even irritated, slightly or a lot, with his or her subject. Sometimes this irritation becomes exacerbated, past annoyance, to something like loathing. Lawrance Thompson's biography of Robert Frost is a notorious example: an "authorized" biography that ends up being almost a diatribe against its subject's character, a denunciation of his weaknesses and faults. This is an extreme example, but there are biographies of giants like Yeats or Rilke for instance, that end up trying to demonstrate that their subjects were so . . . I'd rather not grope for adjectives, but the biographers come to feel, consciously or not, a bit negative, demeaning, subtly diminishing the stature of the poet, asking in so many words how this banal, indeed contemptibly pedestrian personality managed to bring forth evidences of artistic greatness.

This is something that hasn't happened to Whitman. If anything, too many of those who wrote about him came to admire him too much, to believe he was more than a mere poet, but a religious figure, a prophet at least, a kind of Christ. Very early on, from 1866 or so, especially with the publication of William O'Connor's *Good Gray Poet*, which compared Whitman to Jesus, until long after Whitman's death, there are those who all but worship Whitman, and more than a few who write books about him, this prophet, this saint, who in his moral grandeur was Whitman the mortal-immortal, the new link to the metaphysical, the divine, not Whitman the poet.[*] One of his followers, Neil Richardson, after a "meditation session" using *Leaves of Grass* as its text, goes so far as to complain about the "academics": "In turning him into a great poet, they've lost sight of his spiritual dimension."

This is something that rarely but occasionally happens to poets. Blake was self-consciously a prophet, he even called his books prophecies: the task he set himself was to fuse what he considered his purified, revivified religious visions with a renovation of social and historical injustices and misapprehensions, and he had his acolytes, his disciples, too, much like Whitman, if not as many. Rilke had a coterie of mostly wealthy women who came close to adoring him when he was alive, and some of whom did try to make him something like the object of a religious cult after he died. I haven't been able to find out whether it happened to Dante; though he made the most extensive and convincing journey through the realms of poetry

---

[*] A recent book, *Worshipping Walt*, by Michael Robertson (Princeton: Princeton University Press, 2008), is an engrossing study of the many people, from Oscar Wilde to Thomas Eakins, who admired Whitman's spiritual attraction with a sometimes unrealistic fervor.

and religion, there isn't much evidence of his being himself taken as a prophet.

There's no question that even in the first edition of the *Leaves*, Whitman presented himself
quite consciously as something more than a mere
poet, as a kind of savior, who sounds sometimes
perilously close to a Christ, and who at one point
openly identifies with him.

> *That I could forget the mockers and insults!*
> *That I could forget the trickling tears and the*
>   *blows of the bludgeons and hammers!*
> *That I could look with a separate look on my*
>   *own crucifixion and bloody crowning!*

Here, though, after long passages of cosmology
and metaphysics, he addresses again our "you."

> *Not I, not any one else can travel that road*
>   *for you,*
> *You must travel it for yourself . . . .*
>
> *Long have you dreamed contemptible dreams,*
> *Now I wash the gum from your eyes,*
> *You must habit yourself to the dazzle of the*
>   *light and of every moment of your life . . . .*
>
> *I teach straying from me, yet who can stray*
>   *from me?*

*I follow you whoever you are from the present
      hour;*
*My words itch at your ears till you understand
      them.*
*I do not say these things for a dollar, or to fill
      up the time while I wait for a boat;*
*It is you talking just as much as myself I
      act as the tongue of you,*
*It was tied in your mouth . . . . in mine it
      begins to be loosened.*

In a later poem, "To Him That Was Crucified,"
he refers to Christ as "dear brother" and goes on
to establish between them a kind of equality:

*Do not mind because many, sounding your
      name, do not understand you,*
*I do not sound your name, but I understand
      you . . .*

But even earlier than all that, earlier than I'd
like to think, Whitman in fact did refer to his
book as "The New Bible," and he does, even in the
early editions, occasionally use the same term,
and refer to his "prophetic screams." And in "Pro-
toleaf," in 1860 (which later was entitled "Starting
from Paumanok"), he goes so far as to say "*I too,
following many, and follow'd by many, inaugurate*

a new religion." Still, though, for me all of this is a part of his project for the poetry and for that great self the poetry enacts.

Later in his life, when he was surrounded by people who adored him as a prophet as much as a poet, he came rather close to accepting the mantle of a sage whose words went beyond mere wisdom into religious illumination. And he seemed to have had a "magnetic" enough character—a word often applied to him by his admirers—to reinforce this. "The wisest man I ever met," "the man Emerson evoked and prayed for," "not the face of a poet . . . the face of a god," the normally quite solid John Burroughs enthused, and this was restrained compared to the adulation of some of his other admirers. (Burroughs came to mistrust later what he saw as the overglorification of the poet.) Whitman himself knew that reasonable limits were being exceeded, and sometimes said so, but for the most part he took the praise in stride.

It could have turned out badly. In our media-mad age he might have been "exposed," revealed, ridiculed. Back then, though, in those difficult decades before and after the Civil War, the historians speak of a hunger for new modes of spirituality, new prophets, new religions. Whitman had to have been aware of this, and it certainly did color the evolving conception of his work. But he was always basically sane about the part religion had played in his vision, even if some of his followers were not. He appreciated the function religion played in civilization—in the preface to his last prose collection, *Collect*, he writes: "To me, the worlds of religiousness, of the conception of the divine, and of the ideal, though mainly latent, are just as absolute in humanity and universe as the world of chemistry, or anything in the objective worlds"—but the degree to which he actually thought of himself as a religious figure remains highly debatable.

Still, where does that leave us, and me? How much of my admiration for the poems has to do with their aesthetic uniqueness and grandeur, and how much with the promise they make of a new kind of consciousness, indeed a new genre of identity? As a poet, I read with boundless admiration; as a person . . . I don't quite know what to think. How not wish to live in a state of unrestrained acceptance the way the speaker in the *Leaves* does? In the early editions, anyway, before the poet seems to become conscious of being watched, being admired, adored. The way, as I say, he possesses his body, but without avarice, without greed? And puts to use the best part of his intellect not in anything like Socratic skepticism, nor in the endlessly self-dividing analytic scrutiny of our post-Freudian age? Conscious of his community with Americans, then with all humans, then with all gods and all their disciples, yet burning every instant with self-awareness, self-acceptance, self-enlargement?

Does it matter with all this that he is a "great poet"? Isn't this prophetic identity, as the most fervent of his admirers during his lifetime proclaimed—even Wilde, of all people, who didn't much care for Whitman's poetics, pronouncing that his real value was as a prophet—beyond all this? I don't know anymore; I really can't decide. Or even remember how I used to feel about it, because perhaps those first times I read him, it was indeed with a sense of being beyond poetry: now it's more simply that he defines some ultimate reach poetry can have into life.

For all that, it remains his identity as a poet that convinces, not because of his sensitivities, his goodness, his proclamations, his unquestionable spiritual largeness, but almost entirely because of the music, and the vision the music brings forth: as I've said, a poet is defined most distinctly by his or her music, and none, even Hopkins or Dylan Thomas who were both revolutionary, is more comprehensively defined by his music than Whitman. He *is* his music, without it, as in the prose of *Specimen Days,* or *Democratic Vistas,* or *Collect,* he's a sympathetic and often truly wise person, but he's only that. It's his music that compels everything else. Does his work really form the basis for a new religion? The question might be framed by asking if it's the cadences of the Bible that compel belief in its meaning, and the answer is surely not. But it is the music of the *Leaves of Grass* that's absolutely fundamental to our response to it: early on he says it himself, "*Only the lull I like, the hum of your valved voice.*" Without that voice, Whitman might be considered now as just one more nineteenth-century spirituality salesman. With it, he becomes part of the national psyche, and for poets, to a great degree the very foundation of our aesthetic.

I was asked awhile ago whether my work had been "influenced" by Whitman. I answered that rather than being influenced by him or not, for me and possibly most contemporary poets, Whitman is rather our unconscious: he defines for us the project of poetry, its possibilities, its parameters, in a way that's still in effect. It's not necessary to refer to him: he's *there*, always, with that music, that singing, that "Song of Myself," song of us all.

Imagination

If I were to accuse (or possibly praise) Whitman of having generated a text that could be mistaken for the gospel of a religion, it would be a religion of the imagination. Much of the poem is a demonstration of the imagination at work, first in its activity as an acute instrument of perception, then as gatherer of pragmatic evidence of the world, then as a more overtly creative agent of interpretation and transformation.

It's strange to consider the place imagination has had in religion, to notice that the word itself occurs so seldom in religious texts, and finally to realize with dismay that so much of religion seems devoted precisely to a repression of the imagination, to the inhibiting of anything like the free play, free delight of the creative energies of mind that the very word imagination implies. From the ancient founders of religion, to modern self-help pseudo-wise men who have their little time in the public eye, all but a very few religious teachers, and religions, have had at the center of their visions the necessity to still the raucous riot of consciousness, to purify the fantasizing inner mechanism that supposedly torments us with its unruliness. Perhaps that's why so many of the most rigorous fundamental and regressive institutions of religion are so obsessed with demonizing sexuality, because the sexual imagination is both the most difficult to control and the most vivid evidence of what consciousness will do if left to its own proclivities. In the most fanatic of religious sects, even the imagination of the intellect is taken as menacing, for fear of where it might take those who employ it. So Darwin's grand imaginative vision of the past of life on the planet is dangerous because it demonstrates so vividly the wild leaps mind can make towards truth if it's released from conceptual strictures.

With Whitman, there's been a tendency among some critics to transfer even his poetic inspiration to the realm of the religious. Both Malcolm Cowley and Gay Wilson Allen, for instance, use the term "mystical illumination" to refer to Whitman's presumed state of consciousness when he composed the early versions of the *Leaves*. "Mystic," and "mysticism"; many of the commentators from a certain period of criticism threw the term about, although none of them is very clear as to what it might actually mean.

The term "mystical" isn't heard all that much anymore, but in American intellectual culture for a period well on into the twentieth century, it was the highest praise that could be bestowed on an artist or thinker. It was as though the strivings of ordinary human beings were of an inherently lesser nature compared to the exalted, numinous condition of mind implied in this term that touched into and partook of the purity and sanctity of the holy. What was being expressed beneath the surface was a boundless admiration for an accomplishment, the conviction that what had been wrought by the poet, or novelist, or painter, was beyond explication.

There's no doubt that Whitman managed to effect in his poems something that was indeed beyond any "rational" explanation, and the notion of mere inspiration doesn't quite suffice for the awe one can feel for so much of his poetry, for the grandness of its overarching concepts and the radiant details of so many of the lines. The lexicon that describes states of consciousness doesn't contain anything to account for such an outrageously unlikely phenomenon arriving to a normal human being. So perhaps it's not surprising that there would be a recourse to religious locutions to describe his state of mind.

Yet in what's meant to be a compliment also lurks a disparagement: the very grandness of the notion of the "mystical" implies that the strivings of such banal beings as poets or artists are of an inherently lesser worth than the illuminations of the saint or mystic, the qualities and number of which seem infinitely variable. Perhaps this reflexive impulse towards spiritual sanctification had to do with the period of modern history that has been nakedly and bleakly materialistic, but it ends up denigrating imagination, which embodies a much more accurate description of the nomenclature of poetic inspiration than any term tainted with religiosity.

In Whitman's poems, the imagination as an active agent is predominant from beginning to end. Further, Whitman's imagination is one of inclusion, of enhancement, of acceptance and exaltation rather than, as I say, of Rilkean transformation. If there is something like a religious purpose to the work, it is to activate imagination rather than pacify it, to excite consciousness rather than bestill it, to liberate rather than contain it, and, not incidentally, to demonstrate that it isn't only the metaphorizing genius of the poets that can situate us with a blazing awareness in the world. Don't the poems' many addresses to "you" consist almost entirely of promises that they will instill the force and breadth of the imagination in those who properly experience them? And don't they then demonstrate a thousand times precisely that?

Isn't this finally what all art eternally promises us? That it will make our own imaginations more encompassing, and at the same time more acute? When we hear great music, or probably any music, don't we hear it as though it were being generated within us? And don't poems, read properly, come to us in the voice of our own minds?

In no artistic construct more than in Whitman's does imagination truly become an instrument of what might be called a nonreligious redemption: the poems basically offer a vision of imaginative consciousness that is a secular equivalent of the spiritual immortality most religions claim to offer.

Mortality

▨ In what I would very hesitantly call my spiritual life, I don't believe for a moment in immortality, though like all humans I can occasionally find myself reflexively longing towards it. On the other hand, when I give myself over to *Leaves of Grass*, I come marvelously close to having something like an intuition of deathlessness, an experience that blossoms out of the fusion of that primitive instinct to go on forever, with the poetic force of the matter of Whitman's song.

The audacity of Whitman's meditations on and challenges to mortality in the poems is astonishing; they were clearly a key element of his intentions. But what do you do if you seriously want to confront mortality, as a greatest poet, as even, possibly, a prophet? There are so many genres of immortality: the religious, the mythical, the philosophical; even for some scientists the scientific; and there is even in our time a science-fiction immortality, in which sympathetic beings from beyond the stars will transport us into their gleaming spaceships and tend to our temporality and terror.

Whitman proposes an immortality of the poem, of the poet, and the reader. Essentially what he is saying is that if we allow ourselves to participate in the force of his vision, and, surely as important of his singing, his cadence, the swell of his voice and its surge, we will be comforted and solaced even more than by the outmoded precepts of traditional religions. *"The greatest poet . . . drags the dead out of their coffins and stands them again*

on their feet . . . . he says to the past, Rise and walk
before me that I may realize you. He learns the les-
son . . . . he places himself where the future becomes
present."

What Whitman does is overwhelm death with
acceptance, obliterate it with example, with instance, with obsessively reiterated reassurance. In
the section of the 1855 *Leaves of Grass* ultimately
entitled "To Think of Time," but which as well
could be called "To Think of Death," he begins by
speaking of the wonders of mortal existence.

> *To think that the sun rose in the east . . . . that*
> *men were women were flexible and real*
> *and alive . . . . that every thing was real*
> *and alive;*
> *To think that you and I did not see feel think*
> *nor bear our part*
> *To think that we are now here and bear our*
> *part.*

Then he recounts the details of an actual death:

> *When the dull nights are over, and the dull*
> *days also,*
> *When the soreness of lying so much in bed is*
> *over,*

When the physician, after long putting off,
gives the silent and terrible look for an
answer,
When the children come hurried and weeping,
and the brothers and sisters have been sent
for,
When medicines stand unused on the shelf,
and the camphor-smell has pervaded the
rooms,
When the faithful hand of the living does not
desert the hand of the dying,
When the twitching lips press lightly on the
forehead of the dying,
When the breath ceases and the pulse of the
heart ceases,
Then the corpse-limbs stretch on the bed, and
the living look upon them,
They are palpable as the living are
palpable . . .

And after that death enacts a subtle but profound
shift of point of view:

The living look upon the corpse with their
eyesight,
But without eyesight lingers a different living
and looks curiously on the corpse.

Then another death is recounted, in a less generalized, more elaborate way: twenty lines tell of the death of a simple "stagedriver" and elaborate the vivid, ordinary, now poignant details of his very ordinary life. A man who lived with energy, waned, suffered, died. Both these deaths, rendered in such touching detail, with such evident deep sympathy, are like nothing we'd find in Torahs or Korans or Gospels: they are deaths ennobled and in some sense redeemed by imagination.

And subsequent to those deaths, the poem shifts to *pleasure*, of all things, pleasure as a concept that exceeds the concept of morality, and by extension (in its extending) of mortality.

> *The vulgar and the refined . . . . what you call*
> *sin and what you call goodness . . to think*
> *how wide a difference,*
> *To think the difference will still continue to*
> *others, yet we lie beyond the difference.*

And then the pleasure beyond pleasure, which looks out hopefully towards unendingness.

> *To think how much pleasure there is!*
> *Have you pleasure from looking at the sky?*
> *Have you pleasure from poems?*

> *Do you enjoy yourself in the city? Or engaged*
> *in business? or planning a nomination or*
> *election? or with your wife and family?*
> *Or with your mother and sisters? or in*
> *womanly housework? or with the beautiful*
> *maternal cares?*

And the poem and the poet will tell us about where pleasure is taking them, and you, us.

> *These also flow onward to others . . . . you and*
> *I flow onward;*
> *But in due time you and I shall take less*
> *interest in them.*

And if we've been reading attentively, we can recall from "Song of Myself" the first hints of this method of overwhelming, of unlikely convincing.

> *The smallest sprout shows there is really no*
> *death,*
> *And if ever there was it led forward life and*
> *does not wait at the end to arrest it,*
> *And ceased the moment life appeared.*

> *All goes onward and outward . . . . and*
> *nothing collapses,*
> *And to die is different from what any one*
> *supposed, and luckier.*

"Luckier." What possibly can that mean? Yet why does it sound so . . . convincing, so feasible? And later in the "Song":

> And as to you death, and you bitter hug of
>   mortality . . . . it is idle to try to alarm me.

And in "*To Think of Time*" again.

> The sky continues beautiful . . . . the pleasure
>   of men with women shall never be
>   sated . . . . nor the pleasure of women with
>   men . . nor the pleasure from poems . . .
> The earth is not an echo . . . . man and
>   his life and all the things of his life are
>   well-considered . . .

Now one of those passages that, despite my deep disbelief in anything like eternal life, brings me thrillingly close to something like Wordsworth's intimations of immortality, of the possibility of possessing a consciousness able to grasp this overwhelming intuition.

> You are not thrown to the winds . . you gather
>   certainly and safely around yourself,
> Yourself! Yourself! Yourself forever and ever!
> It is not to diffuse you that you were born of
>   your mother and father—it is to identify you,

It is not that you should be undecided, but
that you should be decided . . .

Decided of what? What?

Something long preparing and formless is
arrived and formed in you,
You are thenceforth secure, whatever comes
and goes.

Even one's self?

The threads that were spun are gathered . . . .
the weft crosses the warp . . . . the pattern
is systematic.

Now continues the theme of "preparation."

The preparations have every one been
justified;
The orchestra have tuned their instruments
sufficiently . . . . the baton has given the
signal.
The guest that was coming . . . . he waited long
for reasons . . . . he is now housed,
He is one of those who are beautiful and
happy . . . . he is one of those that to look
upon and be with is enough.

He goes on and on, more and more deaths—"Slowmoving and black lines go ceaselessly over the earth"—more and more vast, convincing promises—"I have dreamed that we are not to be changed so much . . . nor the law of us changed."

And even doubts, so our doubts will be registered, recognized, acknowledged, accepted.

> If otherwise, all these things came out to ashes
>   of dung;
> If maggots and rats ended us, then suspicion
>   and treachery and death.
>
> Do you suspect death? If I were to suspect
>   death I should die now.
> Do you think I could walk pleasantly and
>   well-suited toward annihilation?

And an overcoming again, and a bringing together again of morality and mortality.

> What is called good is perfect, and what is
>   called sin is just as perfect.
> The vegetables and minerals are all perfect . .
>   and the imponderable fluids are perfect;
> Slowly and surely they have passed on to this,
>   and slowly and surely they will yet pass on.

And at last the vision, the culmination of the promise, and the more than delight in the promise.

> *I swear I see now that every thing has an*
> *   eternal soul!*
> *The trees have, rooted in the ground . . . . the*
> *   weeds of the sea have . . . . the animal.*

All accepted, all overwhelmed.

> *I swear there is nothing but immortality!*
> *The exquisite scheme is for it, and the*
> *   nebulous float is for it, and the cohering is*
> *   for it,*
> *And all preparation is for it . . and identity is*
> *   for it . . and life and death are for it.*

The *Leaves* will come back again and again to the challenge of death. In the very next "Sleepers" section, as though remembering:

> *I see nimble ghosts whichever way I look,*
> *Cache and cache again deep in the ground and*
> *   sea, and where it is neither ground or sea.*

And there will be yet another individual death in that section, of a man drowning, told in almost gruesome detail. Yet the demise of one single person, being so profoundly and imaginatively accounted for, allows a kind of immortality to enfold him as well.

Mortality Again

Whitman's vision of death and immortality came to be sorely tested in the years after his first exalted elaborations of them. His brother George was wounded in the Civil War, was sent to Washington to recover, and when Whitman heard about it, he went there and found him. He ended up spending the period of the war and some time afterwards in Washington, working in various government offices and giving over much of his free time helping to care for some of the masses of wounded soldiers who were sent from the grim battlefields to the hospitals. He acted as an unofficial nurse, and something like a psychotherapist to them. "I go sometimes at night to soothe and relieve particular cases," he said in *Specimen Days*, and that was probably the best description of what he did. He was very generous with his time and attention; writing letters home for wounded soldiers, giving them tobacco, tea, or candy, and sometimes even small sums of money, much of which he cadged from women friends in Washington. Later he would add, "I found it was in the simple matter of personal presence, and emanating ordinary cheer and magnetism, that I succeeded and help'd more than . . . anything else."

In the course of his experiences in the hospitals, he was exposed to many gruesome examples of what can happen in combat to the human body and psyche. In "The Dresser" (later titled "The Wound Dresser"), he fictionalizes himself, as he will in many of the other Civil War poems in *Drum-Taps* (first published in 1865, then later much revised), as someone who was dealing much more actively with the wounded than he himself really was. But there's no doubt he had witnessed the sights he records.

> *Bearing the bandages, water and sponge,*
> *Straight and swift to my wounded I go,*
> *Where they lie on the ground, after the battle*
>   *brought in;*
> *Where their priceless blood reddens the grass,*
>   *the ground . . . .*
> *To each and all, one after another I draw*
>   *near—not one do I miss;*

An attendant follows, holding a tray—he
carries a refuse pail
Soon to be fill'd with clotted rags and blood,
emptied, and fill'd again . . . .

The images become more dire as the poem goes
on.

The crush'd head I dress (poor crazed hand,
tear not the bandage away);
The neck of the calvary-man, with the bullet
through and through, I examine;
Hard the breathing rattles, quite glazed
already the eye . . . .

From the stump of the arm, the amputated
hand,
I undo the clotted lint, remove the slough,
wash off the matter and blood . . . .

I dress the perforated shoulder, the foot with
the bullet wound,
Cleanse the one with a gnawing and putrid
gangrene, so sickening, so offensive . . . .

In the prose of *Specimen Days* there are even
more vivid descriptions ("some indescribably
horrid wounds in the face or head, all mutilated,
sickening, torn, gouged out"). Another poem from

Drum-Taps, "The Veterans Vision," is an enactment of what we'd call now posttraumatic stress disorder. It tells of a returning soldier reliving what he had gone through in battle.

> *The engagement opens there and then, in my*
> > *busy brain unreal;*
> *The skirmishers begin—they crawl cautiously*
> > *ahead—I hear the irregular snap! snap!*
> *I hear the sounds of the different missiles—the*
> > *short t-h-t! t-h-t! of the rifle balls;*
> *I see the shells exploding, leaving small white*
> > *clouds—*
> *I hear the great shells shrieking as they*
> > *pass . . .*

Whitman witnessed every manner of dying and death, yet through all the poems of *Drum-Taps*, he never deviates from his sublime convictions about immortality. Though some of the poems come perilously close to sentimentality about the youthful dead, and their bereft families, Whitman never engages in accusation at the injustice of it all, rather he continues as he had in "Song of Myself" to compile examples not of a surrender to suffering, but of his continuing joy in its defiance.

Whitman's most crushing trial, though, came after the war, with the death of Lincoln. To say that Whitman admired Lincoln would be a terrific understatement—he saw the Union itself, America itself, incarnated in him. He would write almost ecstatically about his encounters with Lincoln in Washington, about the two acknowledging one another as they passed in the street. And about Lincoln as a man, as a figure, his praise was without bounds: "The greatest, best, most characteristic, artistic, moral personality," he would say of him; "How quickly that quaint tall form would have enter'd into the region where men vitalize gods, and gods divinify men!" And, on a more personal level: "After my dear, dear mother, I guess Lincoln gets almost nearer me than anybody else."

In 1865 he would commemorate Lincoln's death—without ever mentioning his name; he didn't have to—in one of his most pure, gorgeous lyrics, "When Lilacs Last in the Door-Yard Bloom'd." The poem employs a "trinity," as Whitman calls it, of symbolizations for the structure of its song: the "great star"—Venus, the lilac, and "the thought of him I love." It also uses as connective themes the song of a solitary thrush, which becomes both a reflection of and an embodiment of Whitman singing his poem; Lincoln's coffin; and, not surprisingly, death, personified as a character in its drama; personified twice, in fact, as the "knowledge of death" and the "thought of death."

> *Then with the knowledge of death as walking*
> *   one side of me,*
> *And the thought of death close-walking the*
> *   other side of me,*
> *And I in the middle, as with companions, and*
> *   as holding the hands of companions . . .*

Earlier, death had also fused with the coffin:

> *O death! I cover you over with roses and early*
> *   lilies . . . .*
> *With loaded arms I come, pouring for you,*
> *For you and the coffins of all of you,*
> *   O death . . . .*

And death is personified as a being with its own thoughts and knowledge: "*And I knew Death, its thought, and the sacred knowledge of death.*"

Most crucially, death continues, as it had been in "Song of Myself," to be nothing to be feared, but rather welcomed, and praised. Whitman's imaginative immortality doesn't falter, doesn't blanch before the terrible, difficult task of mourning.

> *Come, lovely and soothing Death,*
> *Undulate round the world, serenely arriving,*
> > *arriving,*
> *In the day, in the night, to all, to each,*
> *Sooner or later, delicate Death.*

> *Prais'd be the fathomless universe,*
> *For life and joy, and for objects and knowledge*
> > *curious;*
> *And for love, sweet love—But praise! O praise*
> > *and praise,*
> *For the sure-enwinding arms of cool-enfolding*
> > *Death . . .*

Whitman finally enlarges and intensifies what is really not merely an acceptance of death, but an exaltation of it.

> *Dark Mother, always gliding near, with soft*
> > *feet,*
> *Have none chanted for thee a chant of fullest*
> > *welcome?*
> *Then I chant it for thee—I glorify thee above all;*
> *I bring thee a song that when thou must*
> > *indeed come, come unfalteringly.*

Approach, encompassing Death—strong
    Deliveress!
When it is so—when thou hast taken them,
    I joyously sing the dead,
Lost in the loving, floating ocean of thee,
Laved in the flood of thy bliss, O death.

The section that includes all this, this cry to "O vast and well-veil'd Death," climaxes and concludes in near ecstasy:

I float this carol with joy, with joy to thee,
    O Death!

It is Whitman's most complete and convincing example of his confrontation with death, and I find to be a statement equal to any religious credo about mortality as a precious human possession, rather than a horror and threat.

The poem itself is about more than even all this. In some ways it's Whitman's most conventional poem, situated in the tradition of poems for a death as occasions for the poet's song. Its closest nineteenth-century relative, at least in its length, would be Tennyson's long elegy and meditation on mortality, *In Memoriam*, which compared to Whitman's wide-ranging, wild threnody seems to plod on forever in predictable metrical variations on its single theme.* All of Whitman's poetic gifts are at work in "Lilacs," and the poem would be the last of his very greatest.

The Sad Captain

▨ Unfortunately, Whitman couldn't leave Lincoln's death alone. He wrote another poem about it, "O Captain! My Captain!" a truly awful piece of near doggerel triteness, which to Whitman's chagrin became his best-known and most popular work, which generations of schoolchildren (including me) would be coerced to memorize. What this has to say about the audience for poetry is too depressing to consider, and it's not necessary to attack the poor poem yet again—it's had enough opprobrium, all of which it merits—and Whitman ultimately regretted publishing it. He said, again to Traubel, "I'm honest when I say, damn 'My Captain' and all the 'My Captains' in my book! This is not the first time I have been irri-

---

* Tennyson was an admirer of the *Leaves*, and the two poets had a brief correspondence. Whitman complimented Tennyson's now mercifully forgotten *Queen Mary* when it was published: did he mean it? Surely it's not only artists who tend to praise those who praise them.

tated into saying I'm almost sorry I ever wrote the poem." He tried halfheartedly to revise it to make it better, or less bad, but the task was hopeless: the poem's conception was a mistake, its execution a disaster. On the other hand, when he was asked as he often enough was to recite it, he did.[*]

Lines

Randall Jarrell in his much esteemed 1953 book of criticism, *Poetry and the Age*, called his essay about Whitman "Some Lines from Whitman," and in fact most of the essay consists of quotations from Whitman: Jarrell mostly writes in a style that

---

[*] A similar though even more grievous story: the great Romanian, German-language poet Paul Celan's "Death Fugue"—"Todesfuge"—which he wrote after the Second World War, and which is almost universally acclaimed as the greatest poem to come out of the Holocaust, as it surely is, came to define Celan's work as irritatingly for him as Whitman's "Captain" had for him, although "O Captain! My Captain" was Whitman's worst poem, and "Todesfuge" was Celan's best. The rest of Celan's work was very different from that poem, in a way less accessible—though there's nothing "easy" about "Todesfuge"—and by the end of his life Celan would no longer read the poem to audiences, nor allow it to appear in anthologies. Celan ultimately killed himself, and it's hard not to wonder whether this might have been a part of it.

might be called "open-mouthed gaping in wonder," a stance that seems to me perfectly appropriate.

Because of Whitman's grand purposes for his poems, their ample design, the uncanny dimensions of their ambitions, and the largeness of their emotions, commentators tend to neglect the brilliance of his ear for the smaller scales of language music, his stunning ability to put together completely unlikely and compelling combinations of words. Often he can be quite subtle in the intricacies of his music, moving through paired vowel patterns: "The clank of the shod horses on the granite floor" or "The armfuls are packed to the sagging mow." But often, too, more often, he devises dances of vowels that can vault the literal meanings of words into sound combinations that create meanings far beyond their utterance. Things like, "the blab of the pave," "lacy jags," "flaunt of the sunshine I need not your bask."

I'll follow Jarrell and quote just a few of my own favorites, some of which I've already cited.

Cold dash of waves at the ferry wharf,
Posh and ice on the river . . .

I see nimble ghosts whichever way I look,
Cache and cache again deep in the ground
*   and sea . . .*

Not you as some pale poetling seated at a desk
　　lisping cadenzas piano . . .

Hefts of the moving world at innocent
　　gambols, silently rising, frankly exuding,
Scooting obliquely high and low.

Smartly attired, countenance smiling, form
　　upright, death under the breast-bones hell
　　under the skull-bones . . .

Delicate sniffs of the seabreeze . . . . smells of
　　sedgy grass and fields by the shore . . . .
　　death-messages given in charge to
　　survivors,
The hiss of the surgeon's knife and the gnawing
　　teeth of his saw,
The wheeze, the cluck, the swash of falling
　　blood . . . . the short wild scream, the long
　　dull tapering groan . . .

(Chilling! You can see him there in the operating chamber listening, and watching, watching, the way his friend Thomas Eakins watched the professor of surgery in his painting *The Gross Clinic*, and the way Whitman himself watches from the balcony in one of Eakins's paintings of boxing matches.)

　　Here are two brief portraits of birds, in poetic figures that go beyond mere personification:

> *The spotted hawk swoops by and accuses*
> *me . . . . he complains of my gab and my*
> *loitering.*
> *Where the laughing-gull scoots by the*
> *slappy shore and laughs her near-human*
> *laugh . . .*

The slappy shore! It seems like an observation most poets would discard as trivial, not sufficiently precise, but Whitman makes it notably precisely in that.

The sea again now:

> *The tempest lulls and the moon comes*
> *floundering through the drifts . . .*

And here's the poet again demonstrating the wildness, the utter unpredictability of his language:

> *Magnifying and applying come I,*
> *Outbidding at the start the old cautious*
> *hucksters,*
> *The most they offer for mankind and eternity*
> *less that a spirt to my own seminal* wet . . .*

We know how to magnify, but to apply? Of course, when you think about it a moment, "ap-

---

* The earliest version has here, an error surely, "semitic."

ply" means to apply the meanings he's discovered, or devised, to the world, to the poem, to us, for us. We just don't think of the word isolated that way, but it works, fiercely.

Jarrell also points out too that Whitman "has at his command a language of the calmest and most prosaic reality, one that seems to do no more than present." And quotes, as I have:

> *The little one sleeps in its cradle.*
> *I lift the gauze and look a long time, and*
> *   silently brush away flies with my hand.*

The contrast between "prosaic" (though it isn't really) moments like this and the flamboyance of often adjacent passages make both tonal realms more effective, more affecting. And, most crucially, they maintain an enduring freshness, a sense of improvisation—more than with any other poet's, Whitman's words sound as though they're being generated as they arrive on the page, spontaneously, with no premeditation, no plotting. How could anyone possibly *plan* to utter "the blab of the pave," or to call the sea "howler and scooper of storms"? There are literally hundreds of examples. This, combined with the way the poems are structured, often with no definite narrative connection between one passage and another, plus the unpredictable evolution of the arguments of the poems, continually reinforces this impression of newness and, to use Whitman's own word, *blurt.*

Every great poet's work, of course, seems at first, and later on, too, something splendidly new: it's one of the most gratifying aspects of living in the world of poems that there should be so many of these revelatory moments. The first time you read a poet of stature, there's a similar surprise and excitement, though with many, in time there comes tempering of enthusiasm, not a turning away from exactly, but a slowing of the racing pulse, a lessening of the feeling of being transported to a new place in one's self. And finally, with some poets, the poets who endure, comes another affirmation, a realizing that even though the initial wonderment has worn off, the poems have become a part of what might be called one's poetic psyche.

With Whitman, at least for me, that second, moderating, reassessment stage doesn't ever seem to occur; I'm moved every time, by excitement, and gratitude. Whenever I turn to the *Leaves of Grass,* the power of the poems is undiminished, the sense of wonder, of something like awe, of transport, not in the least lessened. Naturally there are certain other poets, or other poems by certain other poets, that maintain something of this astounding freshness: Keats's odes, for instance, much of George Herbert, a great deal of Yeats and Rilke; Frost, Larkin, Bishop . . . . In fact, when I stop to think about it, there are really quite a large number, thank goodness. But still, I don't think there's quite the sense with any of them of coming always to them as though for the first time, with the same flood of constant surprise, of something almost like disbelief.

The Voice

In 1992 a celebration of the centennial of the death of Whitman took place at the Cathedral of St. John the Divine in New York; a group of poets came together for an evening to honor Whitman, and we each read passages from the poems. Not long before, a wax cylinder had been discovered on which was recorded the supposed voice of Whitman reading four lines from his short poem "America," and at the end of the event it was played on the public address system. When the poem boomed out over the speakers, a flock of startled swallows, or bats (there's disagreement about which), sped out from dark upper reaches of the nave and flew in a long arc out and then, when the voice stopped, back into their silent darkness. It was very theatric, to say the least.

The recording can readily be found on the Internet now, though if it is indeed Whitman's voice, which, given the sensitivity with which the verse is read, it very well might be, there's still only the most blurred sense of what the actual voice of the poet reading the poems would really have been like, and I think I'm a little relieved.

There are only a few poets I feel this about: Shakespeare, surely, whose poetic voice is so various, so manifold, that no human voice could conceivably contain it; or George Herbert, whose speaking voice couldn't possibly replicate the passionate delicacy of his verses: I think his voice would be too *precise*, somehow, too Englishy, touched with too much material reality. I don't think that about Donne: the voice I hear reading him would be ironized by its accent, the edge of almost playful mockery of human folly in many of the poems would be intensified. I'd love to have heard Keats read; he reputedly spoke with a Cockney accent, which I think would play out in a wonderful counterpoint to his poems' precision and exuberance.

Among the poets who have been recorded over the last century, some of their voices enhance their poems—Eliot, Yeats, Frost, Kinnell—and others seem not to measure up to the work. Stevens sounds pompous, and somehow unserious; W. C. Williams's reading is very flat, and unmusical; Elizabeth Bishop, whose verse music is so sparky, and whose early recordings catch that, towards the end of her life reads in a voice perhaps maimed by decades of tobacco and alcohol, that seems wearied by the sound of itself, for having to perform itself.

Whitman is a special case entirely: it's almost inconceivable to imagine a real voice embodying his incredible range of tone and emotion, the inflective variety, the unlikely linking of timbre. It would be terribly dismaying to hear the passionate sincerity of the work delivered with too much *staginess*, too much operatic pathos. Whitman loved opera, he doted on the flamboyant singers of his time: what if he made the poems sound like the music of Verdi, with a voice like Pavarotti? Unthinkable.

Whitman rarely recited his great poems, claiming, "I don't recite because I don't know them," and, "I never commit poems to memory—they would be in my way." But on one rare occasion when he did, the person to whom he recited afterwards reported, "His voice was strong and sweet."

Life After

Although Whitman labored on and tinkered with and added to and deleted from the *Leaves* his whole life, really the greater part of his last years was spent in reflecting on his earlier inspirations, and living the role of an elder poet with many admirers who considered him as a sage, or as we've seen, a prophet. He seemed mostly pretty happy with the role, welcomed the many visitors who came to be personally in his presence, and answered some of the tide of fan letters he regularly received from a surprisingly large geographical range of readers—most letters, according to Traubel, he would throw away, having first removed the stamps for return postage. Ironically, for someone who had set out to do so much for America, his greatest acclaim for a long time came from Europe: Rossetti, Swinburne,

Ruskin, Stevenson, Wilde . . . . Later, partly as a result of his own self-promotion—something he wasn't at all loathe to do—he would become at home too a celebrity of sorts, though he never really felt appreciated as much as he thought he deserved. There would be, according to Reynolds, "a Whitman cigar, a Whitman calendar, a Whitman tree . . . a Whitman church, and various Whitman societies." And yet he never achieved anything like a broad readership among the ordinary people who were the subject and inspiration of so much of the poetry, and he knew it, and was quietly saddened by it.

He was very debilitated as time went on by the series of strokes that had come to him so prematurely, then near the end by bladder problems, constipation, failing eyesight. Near death, he was in a wheelchair, then mostly in the chair and bed in the bedroom of the small house he'd bought in Camden. He complained of becoming more sensitive to the cold. His room, though, was apparently knee-deep in paper, those unanswered letters, notes for poems, scribbled manuscripts— pleasant to think of him afloat on it all. He never had much money, and when contributions came to him from wealthy friends and admirers, of which he had quite a few, he saved it up for his grand cemetery monument.

He was reputed to be generally very sweet-tempered, and generous with advice to all who visited or attended him. After a period in the 1870s of something like resentment about his lack of success, he seemed to accept it mostly with equanimity, though even when he was quite old, he was unhappy with what he saw as his neglect by a larger public. Sometimes he groused to Traubel. "I was not only not popular (and am not popular yet—never will be) but I was *non grata*—I was not welcome in the world."

But the fantasy of *Leaves of Grass* being finally widely accepted made him laugh a little to Traubel: "I wouldn't know what to do, how to comport myself, if I lived long enough to become accepted, to get in demand, to ride on the crest of the wave. I would have to go scratching, questioning, hitching about, to see if this was the real critter, the old Walt Whitman—to see if Walt Whitman had not suffered a destructive transformation—become apostate, formal, reconciled to the conventions, subdued from the old independence."

If he, as his biographers have pointed out, did in fact compromise somewhat with his early, more radical ideals, becoming more willing to consort with the capitalists he had once mistrusted, not to say despised, and even to write paeans to monarchs, he remained Walt Whitman to the end.

And after the end, as Auden said of Yeats, though perhaps even more so with Whitman, "he became his admirers."

What He Teaches Us

First of all and above all the efficacy of poetry, poetry's power, poetry's redemptive force. He reinforces and in some ways reinvents the elemental fact that poetry is a form of knowledge and a way to truth, that it is a unique genre of aesthetic experience, that it enlarges our conception of and reception of beauty. Whitman's poetry enacts and demonstrates that enlargement, that widening of the lenses of the spirit to absorb and exalt the breadth of our sensitivity and perception.

He could have been a secular preacher, a lecturer and essayist like Emerson: he certainly had enough compelling and original ideas. That he chose poetry as his medium is essential to appreciating what he did: he knew that the way poetry and its music is experienced by consciousness gives it a dimension nothing else can have. He himself learned from the Bible, he learned from the philosophers, from Emerson, but his own real teachers were Shakespeare and Homer above all: other poets of dimension and vision.

His poetry frames his moral argument, organizes it, but also by way of its constantly compelling music, generates it. Morally, what he teaches is to be accepting, to be generous, unselfish; to refuse to reject anyone else's suffering, or pain, or joy either; to not fear sex, to revel in it, all of it, every permutation of it; to desire desire, to not mistrust the demands of the body, nor overvalue the immateriality of the soul, because what we call the soul is so deeply and intricately meshed with the body. He wants us not to be afraid of ourselves, even of our dark, darkest, most doubting selves. To know that the weak and poor and even the patently evil are equal to us by the sheer fact of their existence; the only thing not equal to us is the mob, mindless and taunting. He tells us to take even that into account, though, to take everything into account, to account for everyone and everything we possible can. To be tender with the young, to admire the old, to fear neither age nor death, to exalt in them both. Not to be overawed by god, because in the poems of our spirit we are equal to god; we contain god, old gods and new, and "monstrous sauroids," and endless seas of ever evolving time.

. . . Where stop? It's as though he had taken the Enlightenment and all that came after, all the democratic aspirations, all the modes of revolutionary hope, and turned them to poems, to the person he created in the poems, and at the end to his reader.

But if I employ terms like that, with their edge of polemic, aren't I suggesting that Whitman's identity as a thinker, a prophet, might be as compelling as that of the poet? I've tried to think other poets about whom I'd even entertain this question. Perhaps Dante, who asks us by his construction of a spiritual world counter to ours to be morally more rigorous than we are. And Shakespeare, who demands the same thing by dramatizing our terror, our laughter, our exaltation. Blake more overtly proselytizes us to give over our chains of hypocrisy; Shelley and Byron want us to be more socially, politically, historically staunch. Finally, though, all great poems, by their very definition, by the way they colonize and amplify and enhance the music of our own inner voices, of consciousness and conscience, ask us to be greater than we are, and if we read them well even show us how to begin.

Whitman is in the tradition of those poets who present a view of life inseparable from the methods and matter of their song. But he remains in many ways *our* poet, the poet of our culture, our political and social identity and history. He remains startlingly close to us in his basic concerns: he sees and hears much as we do, but he demonstrates for us how to see and hear more attentively, sympathetically, accurately. Most crucially, in his ever-refreshing, ever-renewing music, he is with us, he is here.

> *I bequeath myself to the dirt to grow from the*
> *   grass I love,*
> *If you want me again look for me under your*
> *   bootsoles.*
>
> *You will hardly know who I am or what I*
> *   mean,*
> *But I shall be good health to you nevertheless,*
> *And filter and fibre your blood.*
>
> *Failing to fetch me at first keep encouraged,*
> *Missing me one place search another,*
> *I stop some where waiting for you.*